God blesseth trewe labour, | Be still quicke and kinde
With plentye and fauour, | Reward thou shalt finde

Pricke not at thy pleasure, | Be watchfull and wise
But in trewe honest measure | In goodwelle to rise

In heaven shall have a place to dwell.

Mrs Groundes-Peace's
Old Cookery Notebook

Mrs Groundes-Peace's Old Cookery Notebook

compiled by Zara Groundes-Peace
edited by Robin Howe

The International Wine and Food Publishing Company
DAVID & CHARLES

A publication of
The International Wine and Food Publishing Company
Marble Arch House, 44 Edgware Road, London, W2

© Rainbird Reference Books 1971

All rights reserved. No part of this publication may be reproduced, stored in a retrieval system, or transmitted, in any form or by any means, electronic, mechanical, photocopying, recording or otherwise, without the prior permission of The International Wine and Food Publishing Company.

This book was designed and produced by
Rainbird Reference Books Limited
Marble Arch House, 44 Edgware Road, London, W2

ISBN 0 7153 5181 8

Printed in Great Britain by Ebenezer Baylis & Son Limited
The Trinity Press, Worcester, and London
Bound by The Dorstel Press, Harlow, Essex

TX
717
.G865
1971

Contents

Editor's Foreword	7
History of Food in Britain	9
Some of the Foods Available in England up to the Eighteenth Century	19
Table Manners	38
Concerning Waffles and Wafers	42
Gingerbread	45
Table Equipment	47
Spoons	47
Forks	48
Knives	50
Nef	52
Salt-Cellars	53
Trenchers and Roundels	56
The Kitchen and its Equipment	59
Old Cookery Books	67
The Forme of Cury	70
Liber Cure Cocorum	71
The Governayle of Healthe	73
The Boke of Kervynge	75
The Castel of Helth	78
Dyets Dry Dinner	80
Via Recta ad Vitam Longam	83
The Closet of the Eminently Learned Sir Kenelme Digbie Kt. Opened	84
Olde Receipts	87
Old English Cookery Glossary	111
Illustration Acknowledgments	125
Select Bibliography	126

FOR RODERICK

Editor's Foreword

Working on the Zara Groundes-Peace manuscript had for me a special flavour. During the summer of 1969 I discovered in a museum catalogue a mention of the small domestic museum in Filkins, Gloucestershire. The old-world name attracted my attention and, the weather being kind, my husband and I drove to this charming Cotswold village – and fell in love with it. The museum proved no less seductive. It was small, housed in a fifteenth-century cottage that once served as the village lock-up, and its curator, George Swinford, who was also its founder, had made it his pride and joy.

Filkins and the museum made a deep impression on me and when I was asked whether I would edit the vast, bulky manuscript of Mrs Groundes-Peace who had lived in Filkins, I felt in some odd way that this had been quietly intended. I could not resist an appeal which came from there.

Back I went to Filkins to discover more about the author of the manuscript. I knew that she had died before she had had time to put her manuscript together. I spoke to her husband, and learned that it was my old friend George Swinford who had lent Zara Groundes-Peace a rare copy of *The Queen's Closet Opened* which had sparked off an interest in ancient cooking receipts, and a serious interest in cookery exploded almost overnight.

George Swinford had, in fact, thought that a chapter in the book entitled *Choice Physical and Chirurgical Receipts* might interest her doctor husband. But the doctor never saw them, for Zara became so involved with the book that it could never be spared for him. She searched the antique bookshops and eventually acquired a copy for herself.

For the next four years – until her death in 1966 – almost all Zara Groundes-Peace's time was devoted to this new absorbing subject, the history of cooking and of English cookery books. She spent hundreds of hours in the Bodleian Library in Oxford and the British Museum in London, and in the smaller museums devoted to the domestic arts. She read everything she could find on her subject, transcribing passages from ancient volumes, many of which the librarians had no recollection of ever having been asked for before. Primitive cutlery, old kitchen equipment, all she had photographed.

Zara Groundes-Peace planned to write an esoteric history of medieval,

Tudor and early Stuart food and its preparation. The second half of the book was to have contained recipes. It was to have been practical as well as academic, with every recipe tried by herself and demonstrated to be practical as well as interesting and appetizing.

Sadly her work was never completed for her death was sudden. Although Zara Groundes-Peace had accumulated an immense amount of material, she had not put it into manuscript form. I can only hope that what I have done with her material is what she would have liked to have seen. I think Zara Groundes-Peace had probably anticipated a larger book, but for me to have done this would, I believe, have detracted from its present charm. Although Zara Groundes-Peace did not herself finish her work, I am sure she derived enormous pleasure in the busy last four years she spent delving into old manuscripts; her evident enjoyment comes through the letters which were among her papers. These were letters to the curators and keepers of famous libraries who, it seems, never hesitated to assist in searching for these ancient volumes, nor minded how many times they were photographed. She must have enjoyed her travels to the many small yet fascinating museums, and I think she had no doubt in her mind that one day her book would be published. That I have been able to edit this manuscript has given me great pleasure.

R.H.

History of Food in Britain

No one should overrate man's impulse to eat, an impulse which takes precedence over the sex impulse and other pleasure impulses. First man ate to live; then, if one judges by early descriptions of the food of the rich, man lived to eat. Finally, but much later, man learned to eat for pleasure as well as to live.

The inhabitants of this island at the time of the Romans were, according to the testament of the Roman Diodorus Siculus, a people of simple eating habits. In fact, the Romans had a poor opinion of their food resources. The staple diet of the people of Britain was the flesh of sheep and oxen. They had neither butter (this came much later, and although butter was often mentioned in the Bible this may well have been curds) nor oil. They cultivated grain in small patches and when this ripened pounded it into a paste. They did not believe that hares, hens or fish were worth eating; actually they regarded them all with intense suspicion. A dull manner of eating compared with the culinary exoticism of the Romans.

Whether or not the Romans tried to influence the Britons one does not know, although it is a curious fact that no Roman culinary influence is found in our cooking today. But the Romans did not neglect the country they occupied for 367 years. They cleared forests and improved husbandry. They imported the foods they liked into the country, 'from cherries to snails'. It is said it was the Roman Legionaries who unconsciously planted the wild cherries which still grow along the sides of those old marching roads. As the soldiers marched, they munched cherries, throwing out the stones.

To the Romans we also owe the introduction to this country of mulberries, plums, quinces, figs and vines. Wherever the climate permitted the Romans planted vineyards, and even produced wines, although really good wines they imported from abroad. Vineyards later became a characteristic of the great Catholic religious houses and considerable quantities of wine, both red and white, were made. It was in Tudor times that the decline of the vineyards took place.

The Romans gave us walnuts, filberts, chestnuts and many of the vegetables we think of as very English: peas, cucumbers, leeks and onions, potherbs and the like.

Well might the Romans have had a low opinion of British eating habits and their food resources – with one notable exception, our oysters. These were already prized by the Roman gourmets long before the Roman occupation of Britain. Indeed, their reputation was so well established that Sallust, the historian, writing in 50 BC said loftily: 'The poor Britons, there is some good in them after all, they produce an oyster.' As the Romans were pioneers in oyster cultivation they probably did much to improve oyster cultivation in Britain.

For a time after the arrival of the Saxons, good eating suffered a setback, but once the Saxons had established their right to remain in Britain, they too settled down to good husbandry, bringing among other things rye to this country. It remained for long the cereal from which the bread of the people was made.

The Saxons enjoyed life and lived it to the full when they were not at war or hunting. Much of the rest of their time seems to have been spent in gourmandizing. Festive gatherings were reputed to be more frequent than among any other race. They spread their tables with cloths and sometimes had silver dishes and drinking vessels. On the table was placed beef, sheep's flesh, pig, goat, calf, deer, hart, wild boar, peacock and swan. They ate also pigeons, wildfowl, barnyard fowl and other birds. They were fond of salmon, eels, hake, pilchards, trout, lampreys, periwinkles, lobsters, plaice,

Spit-roasting: different meats were cooked at varying distances from the fire, and the meat was brought straight from the spit to the table.

sole and sprats. The cooks made broths, junkets and oyster patties; they also stuffed chickens. Meat was cooked and served on spits. They ate apples, peaches, pears and plums, medlars and cherries.

The Saxons were fond of pot-herbs. According to records of the period before the Norman conquest, long lists of herbs were kept in England together with their uses. 'If then thou will that thy meat easily melt, take then betony the wort three drachams in weight, and of honey one ounce; seethe [boil] them the wort till it harden; drink them in water two cups full.'

They liked good quality food, stone-ground flour to make their bread, and their meats well spiced; they knew quite a lot about the making of salads and in particular seemed to have liked watercress. Cheese, honey – which they also used for sweetening – and oatcakes were eaten. They drank plenty of mead although this in those days was the drink of the rich rather than the peasants. It was made from one part honey boiled with four parts water – pure water being specified. Mead was a favourite drink of Queen Elizabeth I. A similar drink called metheglin was preferred in Wales, flavoured with herbs and fermented with yeast. Of the Welsh and their drink Dr Thomas Cogan once wrote: 'It is as natural a drinke for them as Nectar for the Gods. And I have heard some of that nation defend that it is the verie Nectar which Jupiter and Juno dranke.'

The coming of the Danes or Vikings to our island scene brought ever

A variety of herbs being prepared for the still.

harder drinking and greater excesses of eating. King Hardicanute, an egrarious glutton, was famous for his gourmandizing and unrestricted hospitality. Four or five times daily his table was set for eating and all were welcome to sit at it. But like other greedy men before and since, Hardicanute fell a victim to his excesses while attending a wedding feast in Lambeth, and was dead several days later. It is recorded that he died because he swallowed too big a draught of wine without taking the goblet from his lips. For many years the anniversary of this famous glutton's death was celebrated under the appropriate name of Hogg-tide. Another Dane, Prince Guthrun, rejoiced in the nickname Gormandus. An unusual Danish custom was that of eating on alternate days fish with milk, and flesh with ale, perhaps to counteract over-indulgence.

With the Norman Conquest came Norman manners and Norman food, and certainly this influence has stayed with us. These conquerors by comparison with their predecessors were dainty eaters. But they too liked plenty of spices for obvious reasons, to disguise the general staleness of their meat. They introduced ceremony with feasting. Boar's head and peacock were served to the blare of trumpets although the Normans were content with two meals a day unlike the Saxons.

The Bayeux Tapestry illustrates the feast given by William the Conqueror before the Battle of Hastings. It shows meat being cooked in a bag, possibly the skin of the animal being cooked. We can see joints of meat and poultry on spits. Loaves of bread are being taken from the oven on two-pronged forks. The nobles are sitting at the table, one is eating fish, others are drinking. Grace is being said and the Conqueror is being offered a bowl of water for his ablutions and a napkin on which to dry his hands.

William the Conqueror liked feasting and so he had himself crowned three times in one year and on each occasion gave a feast. We say 'he gave a feast' but actually his feasts impoverished the whole kingdom. He celebrated festivals with suitable feasts: Christmas at Gloucester, Easter at Manchester, and Whitsun at Westminster. He was said to be particularly fond of roast crane, and once, when he was served only half a roasted crane, he had to be forcibly restrained from striking the steward. His overeating and obesity were the indirect cause of his death.

William's overeating habits seem to have been inherited by at least one of his sons, Henry I, who it is recorded died from a fit of indigestion brought on by eating a surfeit of lampreys. These pseudo-fish with no scales and looking like an eel were a great favourite among medieval gourmets and gourmands, and in such demand that King John issued a mandate to the Sheriffs of Gloucester forbidding them, on the first coming in of the lampreys, to sell them for more than two shillings each. Gloucester was famous for its lampreys, the best of which were found in the River Severn (there were at one time said to be large numbers in the Thames). Gloucester was also famed for its method of cooking them. One wonders whether the Gloucester cooks used an old recipe which gave instructions on 'how to fry, broil and roast a live lamprey at the same time'. Another Gloucester custom was the presentation to their sovereign every Christmas of a lamprey pie as a token of their loyalty. It is odd they should have chosen Christmas to make their presentation pie since lampreys were at their dearest at this time of the year (which could have meant they wanted to prove doubly their loyalty) and also, since they were not in season, they were not at their best. According to *The Boke of Kervynge* (see page 75), the correct way in which to refer to a lamprey when dealing with it at table is to say, 'string that lamprey'.

It was at this period in our history that people were beginning to take a new interest in food. Despite the excesses of William and his son Henry, the Normans on the whole were epicures and the households of the nobles were better planned. Housewives kept good accounts of their household expenditures and of what they cooked and ate. The first cookery books were being written and produced, many of which have survived and make fascinating reading. We have complete lists of foods available at the time and discover that great quantities of meat and fish were eaten, salt fish and herrings in particular. Our Norman ancestors drank ale, beer, wine and cider. It is from the Normans we get our simnel cake and a dish of fried bread and milk curiously called 'The Poor Knights' or in French *pain perdue*. Their bakers baked both white and spiced breads. They liked goose, pease potage and rye bread and cheese. Among the fish listed are whitebait, eel and conger eel, salmon (which at one time was cheap) and lampreys. Whale was also eaten.

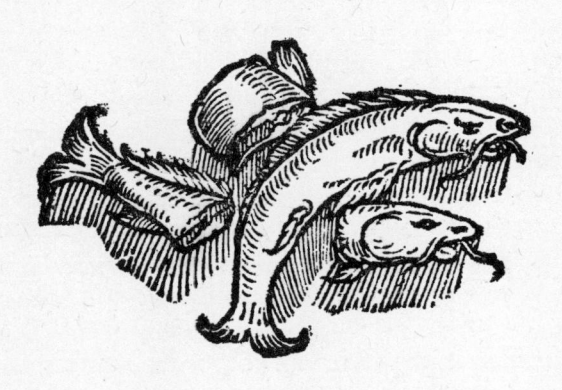

Although the list of fish in medieval times is impressive, the supply of fresh fish to inland towns was obviously limited. Nevertheless, where it was available, fish was popular. Much of it was salted as this made for easier transportation, and the English salted fish was reckoned as some of the best. Most of it was cured in the fishing grounds, and quantities of salted and pickled fish were also imported from Norway. There was considerable trade in herrings both salted and pickled. London's fresh fish came from the rivers and streams, much of it from the Thames. Some freshwater fish, such as carp and pike, were kept in artificial ponds. Oysters were cheap and were 'cried' in the streets.

Great care was taken with the sale of fish. Fish markets were well controlled and evil-smelling fish, which was considered to cause epidemics, was quickly confiscated, taken outside the city and burnt.

We owe much to the culinary interest and skill of the monks in the great religious houses whose kitchens became strongholds of medieval cooking. In their orchards and gardens the monks grew all the existing fruits and vegetables, often improving on them, also introducing new crops. But even in the monastery gardens not many vegetables were grown. Rich and poor alike took little interest in them. They ate onions, always so popular that they were imported in lean times from neighbouring Flanders, garlic and leeks, and a variety of pot-herbs. Among these are some we still recognize, such as sage and rosemary, and others which we regard as roadside plants, like wild fennel, bugloss, borage etc. These herbs were grown not only to give additional flavour to the somewhat insipid food but also for health reasons.

There appears to have been enough fruit, but only during the summer months. Although fruit in general was well liked, it was not approved by some writers, like Sir Thomas Elyot, who wrote in his *Castel of Helth* (see page 78), 'Fruites generally are noyfulls to man, and do engender ylle humours'. He had a kind word though to say of peaches, 'they do make better juyce in the bodys for they are not too soone corrupted beyng eaten'.

However, King John is said to have died from overeating peaches and drinking new cider at the same time. But not much attempt was made in the cultivation of fruit trees and the general quality of fruit was poor. Not until Queen Elizabeth I's time did fruit and vegetables begin to improve. This was due to the influx of refugees fleeing from the Duke of Alva. Apart from apples, pears, plums etc., 'shell' fruits which mean walnuts, hazelnuts and even chestnuts, were listed under fruit.

By Tudor days considerable quantities of livestock were kept by the rich and the better-off peasants. There were draught cows and oxen, pigs and poultry. Even so, little was known about husbandry and the quality of the meat was poor. Pigs and poultry were expected to scratch for themselves and were seldom fed. At all times the poor snared animals in the woods and poached birds from the air, although the punishment for poachers was severe.

Spices continued to be used in great quantities which must have neutralized the flavour of most of the food. However the latter would have tasted less putrid than was otherwise inevitable. Meat particularly needed spicing, and much washing in vinegar before it was fit for the table. Undoubtedly the use of these spices was also medically sound and probably saved many a life. Spicery meant cinnamon and canel (see Glossary), nutmeg, mace, cloves, pepper and of course saffron. Also included in the term spicery were sugar, almonds, dates, figs and raisins. Spices were so important that in royal and noble houses there was a Clerk of the Spicery, and under him a Yeoman Powderbeater whose task no doubt was to grind the spices for daily use.

Saffron was held in the greatest esteem, and in England large quantities of it were grown in the Essex town of Saffron Walden to which saffron gave its name; *walde* is the Anglo-Saxon word for field. But although saffron was a home product, it was still an expensive item costing as much as imported cinnamon. Saffron was never an easy crop, but because it was considered a cure against fevers and the like, the saffron trade flourished.

Soups and potages began to appear on the daily menus although it seems that soup was first officially mentioned on a bill of fare at the wedding of Henry IV. Dr Andrew Boorde, writing in the sixteenth century, said, 'Potage is not so moch used in al Crystendom as it is used in England.' Favourite soups were pease potage and a sort of 'grewell', and a soup they called 'almon mylke'. Fennel was a favourite flavouring for soups. It is perhaps odd that none of the English soups have become world classics.

Gradually the tables of the rich became more interesting. Bread was made with fine wheaten flour, imported French and German wines were drunk; game and venison were roasted, pork and veal, and more and more fish was served. There were many salads made with a variety of green 'saladings' and dressed with olive oil and wine-vinegar. There were dried fruits, raisins and prunes etc., coming in from the Levant and Spain.

Cows were still small and used for draught rather than milk, which could not in any case be kept long. When it was available, the price was comparatively low. Instead of milk, 'almond milk' was used, made from finely pounded almonds mixed with wine and water. There was not much butter and what there was quickly went rancid. During the winter it was salted. Much of it was frequently sold in a semi-liquid state and does not sound appetizing. The fat from chickens and other poultry was used in cooking.

E. Kidder's
RECEIPTS
OF
Pastry
AND
Cookery,

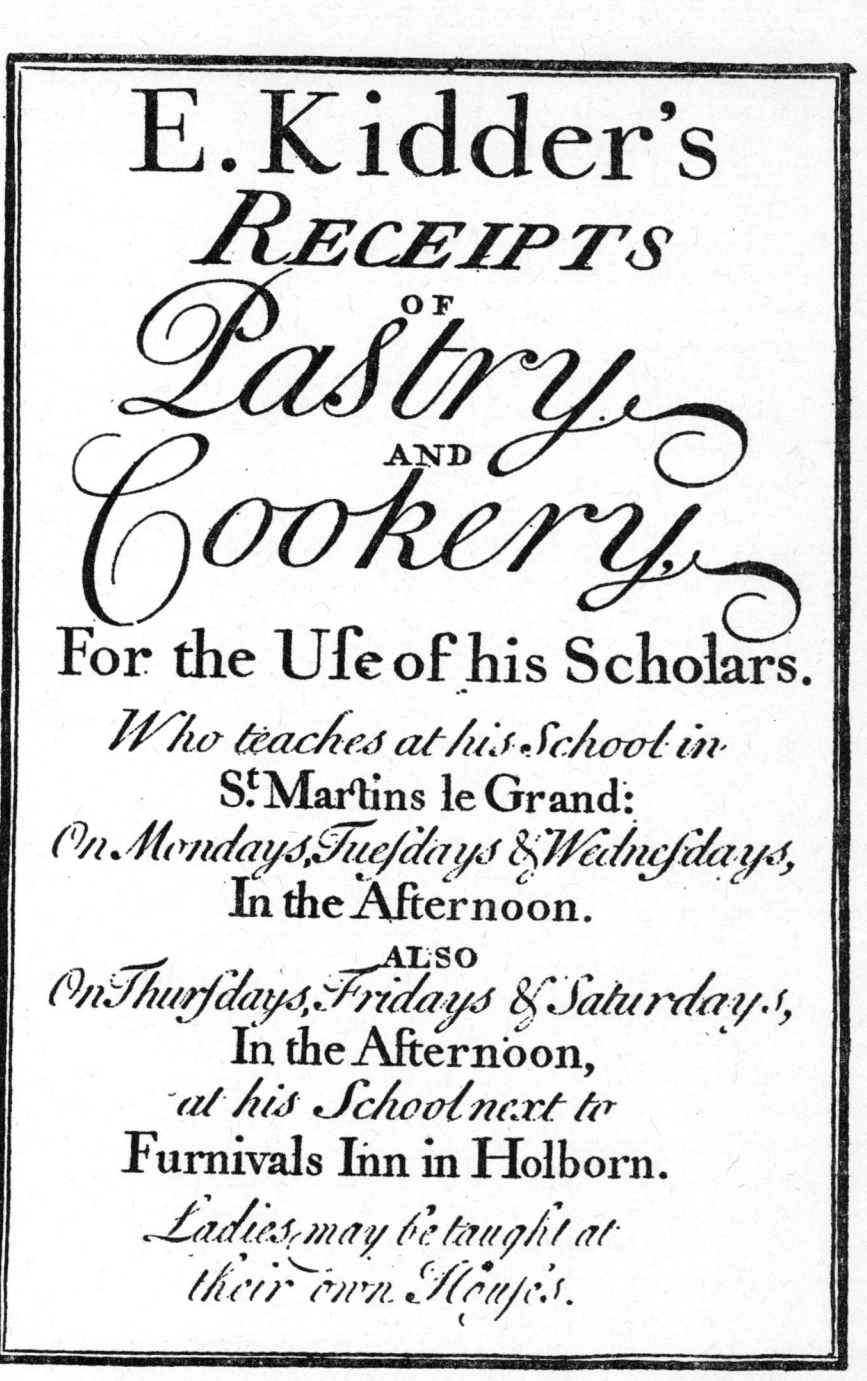

For the Use of his Scholars.

Who teaches at his School in
St Martins le Grand:
On Mondays, Tuesdays & Wednesdays,
In the Afternoon.
ALSO
On Thursdays, Fridays & Saturdays,
In the Afternoon,
at his School next to
Furnivals Inn in Holborn.
Ladies may be taught at
their own Houses.

Interest in the appearance of food gave rise to schools of cookery. This is the title page from an early cookery course.

Honey was still used for sweetening. But in the fifteenth and sixteenth centuries cane sugar was imported from India and Arabia by way of Venice. This was used mainly for making 'marchpanes' or marzipan and other sweetmeats. A large number of recipes called for sugar, even for savoury dishes. However, the amount of sugar used in savoury dishes was not great, rather in the quantity the Italians today use sugar with tomatoes. But even so, some of the sweet-savoury dishes of those days appear to modern palates as positively nauseating.

Market gardening began to improve and with it the range of vegetables increased to include cabbages, peas and parsnips, spinach, carrots, potatoes (they came late into English cooking), and vegetable marrows – these were also used to make sweet dishes. Rhubarb was used as a medicine for 200 years before it appeared as a dish of stewed fruit. There were still no tomatoes, bananas, coffee, tea, brandy, or for that matter gin or whisky.

Bread was still very much the staff of life, and the ovens in which it was baked were communal. Only very large households had their own ovens. Home-baking generally meant food baked on the hearth, like oatcakes. The type of baking that we understand today, where food rises in the oven, was literally unknown. The only items of bakery were bread and pastry. Chemical rising agents were obviously unknown (they were first used in the mid-nineteenth century). To bake a cake, it was necessary to beat the mixture by hand for a matter of an hour or so.

Boiled puddings also are comparatively late arrivals on our culinary scene, becoming popular only in the seventeenth century with the arrival of cheaper sugar. There were types of haggis-puddings (the Romans were the inventors of haggis). Regional biscuits and cakes do not appear in the early recipe books. Shrewsbury Biscuits first appeared in 1620, the same time as Banbury Cakes. Cakes of the Tudor period appear to have been what are today termed biscuits in Britain, and the so-called Tudor biscuits are what we call a cake today.

By Queen Elizabeth I's time, people were experimenting with foods. Many dishes were not only spiced but also perfumed. Flowers were much used in cooking. Roses were candied or made into jam and jellies. Gillyflowers and rose-buds were combined to make a salad, or violets mixed with cowslips. The mixtures were sprinkled with wine-vinegar and chopped fresh herbs. Marigolds, elderberries and barberries helped to give perfume to many dishes.

With the growing interest in cooking and daintier eating, emphasis began to be placed on the appearance of the dishes, and many were the curious terms used to describe them. Dishes were 'flourished', 'strewn', and 'gilded'. The gilding was often done with gold leaf and it is from the gilding formerly given to gingerbread that we get the expression 'the gilt on the gingerbread'. Other dishes were 'endored' (made gold) with egg yolk. Saffron was popular for colouring all kinds of food, sweet and savoury.

Wine was served instead of water; it was much safer for the water supply was often contaminated. Large quantities of wines from Bordeaux, or Gascony, as it was then called, were dispatched from France. It was this English demand that laid the foundation of the great Bordeaux wine trade.

Most of the food eaten before the introduction of forks from Italy (see page 49) was mashed or pounded in a mortar for easy eating, and it was eaten mostly with a spoon or with the fingers. On the whole people had bad teeth and, even if provided with a fork, would have found chewing difficult.

Many of the medieval dishes were made with a basis of bread sauce. Breadcrumbs, almonds and rice flour (pounded rice) were used to thicken dishes. This might well have been because it was often too hot to approach the fire near enough to follow the modern instruction of 'gradually stir in the flour'. But breadcrumbs are still popular in Britain today. We have our bread puddings and bread sauces, and even our sausages, some say, are more bread than meat!

Writing shortly after the death of Queen Elizabeth I, Fynes Moryson said: '... venison pasty is a dainty rarely found in any other kingdom. No kingdom in the world hath so many dove-houses. Likewise brawn is a proper meat to the English, not known to others.'

English cooks were already being commended for their roast meats, and legend has it that it was our roast beef on which the Elizabethan sailors were fed before they went into battle to dispatch the Spanish Armada.

But myths die hard, and we will probably remain convinced that our ancestors ate splendid roast beef as often as they liked.

Some of the Foods Available in England up to the Eighteenth Century

It is not easy to discover decisive evidence of what was actually eaten in medieval days and up to the seventeenth and eighteenth centuries, despite the many cookery books of the period and a mass of old writings. Some people feel that there was a culinary renaissance in Elizabethan days; others bewail that much of the medieval magnificence died with the coming of the Tudors. The Reformation brought many sobering culinary changes; a great number of feast days was abolished and puritanism expressed itself as in the couplet:

> *Plum broth was Popish, and mince-pies –*
> *Oh, that was flat idolatry.*

Sometimes the picture we get is confusing. The rich gourmet of the fourteenth century paid high prices for such delicacies as 'morsels of whale', porpoise or sea-wolf, grampus, and, of course, eels. In the British Museum's Harleian manuscript is a fifteenth-century recipe (No. 279, recipe 40) for a Puddyng of Purpayese, a dish which was served as late as the time of Henry VIII and indeed at the royal table. It reads as follows:

> 'Take the blood of him and the grease of himself and oatmeal and salt and pepper and ginger and mill these together well and then put this in the gut of the porpoise and then let it seethe easily and not hard a good while and then take him up and boil him a little and then serve forth.'

By the eighteenth century they were calling for 'ragoût of fatted snails, and "chickens not two hours from the shell".' Morsels indeed!

From old London ballads we know that 'stockfish, salt fische, whyt herring rede herring, salt salmon, salt sturgeon, salt eels' were all eaten. There was also a good deal of salt meat, giving the people the curse of scurvy, a trouble which lasted until the beginning of the eighteenth century. But meat had to be salted since there was no provender for cattle in those days of ignorance of winter husbandry. So, at each Martinmas, large numbers of cattle were slaughtered and salted down for the winter.

With the Tudors came new discoveries in foods, many of them introduced by returning travellers. The old couplet tells us:

Gourmet foods of the sixteenth century: turtle, snail, frog and artichoke.

> Turkeys, carp, hops and beer
> Came into England all in one year.

And that year was 1520. Turkeys came from Mexico, hops were brought over from the Continent. Carp, however, was known in medieval times and had probably declined in popularity before it made a come-back.

A good source of culinary information is culled from the London street cries of the period. For example:

> Then unto London I did me hye,
> Of all the land it beareth the pryse:
> 'Hot pescodes!' one began to crye,
> Strabery rype, and cherryes in the ryse;
> One bad me come nere and by (buy) some spyce,
> Peper and safforne they gan me bede,
> But for lack of mony I myght not spede.
> Then went I forth by London Stone,
> Throughout all Canwyke Streete,
> Drapers mutch cloth me offred anone;
> Then comes me one cryed, 'Hot shepes feete';
> One Cryde 'Makerell,' 'Rysters grene,' an other gan greete;
> One bad me by a hood to cover my head,
> But for want of mony I myght not be spede.

Or:

> *Cooks to me they took good intent*
> *And proffered me bread, with ale and wine,*
> *Ribs of beef, both fat and full fine.*

There appears to have been plenty of food available in the city, and in most parts of the countryside as well, although of a somewhat rude quality. Londoners had a reputation for being gluttons. Stowe, writing in 1598, says: 'The cooks cried hot ribs of beef roasted, pies well baked and other victuals. There was a clattering of pewter pots, and harp, and pipe and sawtrie.'

And what a clatter that must have been, as the hawkers peddled pots and pans and other kitchen utensils through the narrow streets and lanes, each with his own cry. Pies and puddings have given some London streets their name. There was Pudding Lane and Pie Corner, and of the latter it was written: 'Pigges are al houres of the day on the stalls piping hot, and would crie (could they speak) "Come eat me, eat me!"'. Roast pork was famous in the city and that sold at Bartholomew Fair, a 'Barthemy pig', was considered the very finest. Incidentally, the Great Fire of London started in a bakery in Pudding Lane and devastated hundreds of streets and homes before it stopped at Pie Corner, thus causing the poor to declare that the fire was an act of God punishing them for their greed and vice.

By the beginning of the seventeenth century oranges and lemons were being cried on the streets:

> *Fine Sevil oranges, fine lemmans, fine;*
> *Round, sound, and tender, inside and rine,*
> *One pin's prick their virtue shew:*
> *They've liquor by their weight, you may know.*

Since these were bought from our erstwhile and determined enemy, Spain, this was, as F. W. Hackwood wrote, 'a triumph of trade over war'.

Great meat eaters though the English were, the standards of butchery were low and it was complained that the streets of London were being polluted from the 'corrupt airs' coming from the slaughterhouses. Complaints were so loud that butchers were eventually forced to do their slaughtering outside the city walls.

Vegetables were still not popular, potatoes had not yet been grown for human consumption, kitchen gardens produced more herbs than regular vegetables, and even many of the fruits we know today scarcely existed. There were, however, strawberries, and it is said that we owe the eating of this fruit with cream to Cardinal Wolsey. We imported cherries from

Flanders, despite their earlier introduction by the Romans, and it was not until Henry VIII's gardener, John Tradescant, started to encourage their cultivation that people thought much about this delicious fruit.

By the close of the sixteenth century, however, certain areas were beginning to make a reputation for home-produced foods. There was Cambridge butter, Suffolk milk, Cotswold mutton, and Hampshire pork, Buckinghamshire bread and Gloucestershire cheese. Cornwall boasted of its pies, Kent was known for its hops, Middlesex for its cherries, Worcestershire for pears, Lancashire for beans, and Nottinghamshire for beer. Both Gloucestershire and Herefordshire claimed the distinction of producing the finest apples. Bedfordshire grew barley which produced a high quality malt, and the men of that county were dubbed 'malt-horses', in the same manner the pig-breeding men of Hampshire were called 'hogs'. Lancashire produced the finest and biggest kine (cows), while Essex earned a reputation for its calves.

Fish was highly thought of, as always. The Thames had fine salmon and smelt, the Severn produced excellent salmon in abundance, the Fen country was highly rated both for its wild fowl and fish, while the pike of Wytham and the Ancholm eels were prized, as indeed were those lampreys from the Severn. The style of cooking was changing, plain roasts and boiled meats fought and won a hard battle against the earlier elaborate dishes. Meat and vegetables were cooked together to make a 'hotpot' and turned out on to a large platter. Mutton and beef were frequently on the table. Potatoes, when they were finally accepted, were eaten only with roast beef.

F.W. Hackwood wrote: 'By the time of the Georges the culinary art had sunk as low as the apple-dumpling, the making of which puzzled the thick head of "Farmer George":

> How? cried the staring monarch with a grin –
> How the devil got the apple in?'

But the people were still using spices, saffron and 'cochineli' or 'blew starch', or the juice of flowers such as violets, gillyflowers and marigolds for colouring sweet dishes. To give perfume to their dishes they liked to use musk, civet, rose-water, orange-water and even violet-water.

Tea and coffee, although known in the seventeenth century, were still too expensive, and even children drank beer. Breakfast for most people would be a mug of beer and some bread with butter. And, thinking of breakfast, a meal which today in England is almost unthinkable without marmalade, the sixteenth century reintroduced quince, called by the Portuguese name *marmelo*. From this was made a conserve called marmalade. Quinces and oranges were frequently cooked together to produce a preserve they called 'orangdow'.

The following list gives a fair idea of what our ancestors ate and at what period in time the different vegetables appeared, and often disappeared only to be reintroduced into the diet of the people. It is certainly interesting to discover how vegetables accepted as being very English were, in fact, importations from other countries.

ALE Lays claim to a hoary antiquity. Certainly it was known in ancient Britain. Ale and beer were synonymous terms until Tudor days.

ALMONDS Planted in England in 1548 and cultivated fairly extensively but although the trees blossom freely they seldom reach the fruit stage, even today.

ANISEED Used since the time of Henry III.

APPLES Probably introduced into England by the Romans. The oldest English apple is the Permain, the earliest recorded by Norfolk in 1200. The Luttrell Psalter (1340) has among other fascinating drawings one of apple stealing. Costard apples, which were a distinct fruit, cost 1/- per 100 in 1296. The word costermonger comes from the seller of costard apples. Apple Johns were a late-ripening apple at its best when shrivelled and withered. They were noted for their long-keeping properties. Old people were described as 'withered like an Apple John'. Pippins were introduced by Leonard Maschal in the sixteenth year of Henry VIII's reign.

APRICOTS These reached England by the thirteenth century, probably via Italy, carried here by the returning Crusaders, although some think they were originally introduced by the Romans and suffered an eclipse under the Anglo-Saxons. The Tudors called them apricocks. Although generally known in England by 1540, one of the earliest recorded apricot plantings was by Wolf, gardener to Henry VIII in 1524. Shakespeare makes the gardener in *Richard II* talk of 'yon dangling apricocks'.

ARTICHOKES Related to the common thistle, artichokes were brought from Italy and planted in England in 1548 and at one time grew so well they were exported to the Continent. They were common by 1596 but little favoured and were nearly all lost in the severe winter of 1739–40. They were grown at Holyrood Castle, Edinburgh, in 1683. The Jerusalem artichoke was introduced in 1617 or 1620 and was common by 1629. The name of the latter is supposedly an odd corruption of the Italian name *girasole* or sunflower which, the Italians felt, it resembled.

ASPARAGUS Wild asparagus is a native of Lincolnshire, Essex, Wales, Cornwall and Dorset, and common on the coasts of those regions. It was considered to promote the appetite and so served at the beginning of a meal. It was used in 1559 and thereafter. Pepys mentions his love of this vegetable.

BACON Probably used in medieval times together with eggs as there was plenty of both.

BANBURY CAKES A pastry cake and a speciality of the town of Banbury, Oxfordshire.

BARBERRIES Berberis; indigenous to Britain especially near Colnbrook, the site of London's major airport just west of the capital, and in the north of England. It was used in pickles and for making a syrup and lozenges.

BEANS Three kinds of bean, the haricot, kidney and French were introduced into England from Holland about 1509. Scarlet runners came later, either in 1548 or 1633. However, excavations from the early Iron Age show that a small kind of broad bean was cultivated at that period.

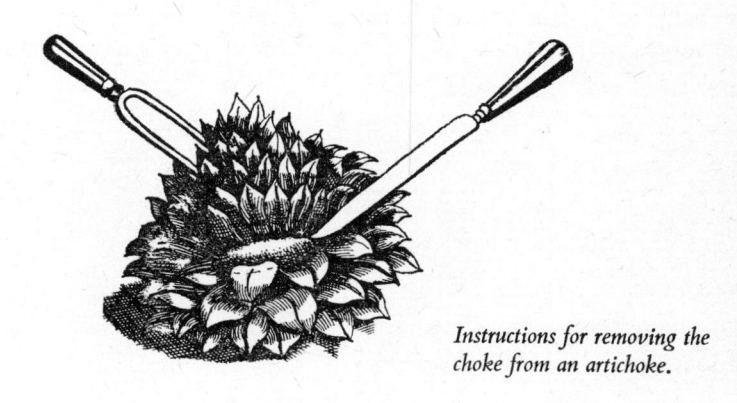

Instructions for removing the choke from an artichoke.

The private room of a Jacobean alehouse.

BEER Under the Normans, beer (or ale) cost 1d. for two gallons in London and ½d. in the country. The manor houses brewed prodigious quantities of beer, much of which was sold to the village ale houses. Later beer was brewed by most farmers as well as by innkeepers and in hostelries. By Tudor times there were many breweries; in Aberdeen alone in 1569 there were 153. Some of the old breweries, like Meux, date back to the seventeenth and eighteenth centuries.

BEETROOT This existed in England as early as 1578, but as a vegetable it was well known to the ancients.

BOAR'S HEAD Wild boar was certainly eaten in Saxon times and the Normans elevated it to a festival dish. But the animal became extinct in Britain in the seventeenth century.

BORAGE Known as bugloss in Queen Elizabeth I's time when both the leaves and the flowers were eaten.

BRANDY This came into use in the seventeenth century and was a favourite drink among the upper and middle classes.

BRAZIL NUTS These were used from the time of Henry III.

BROCCOLI Introduced in the fifteenth century from Italy, where it was a favourite Roman vegetable.

[26]

BUTTER This was used in cooking more than at the table. Much of it was rancid. It was made in early summer and May butter was considered the best.

CABBAGE Known since 1440, it was also called cole, colewort, kale, seacale or sea colewort. A cabbage carved in stone lies at the foot of Anthony Ashley's tomb, Wimborne St Giles.

CAKE The Oxford English Dictionary gives 1579 as the first mention of cake, but Tusser talks of Seede Cake in 1477.

CAPERS Also called caphers, these were eaten in abundance in the time of Queen Elizabeth I.

CAPSICUM Cultivated in England in the reign of Edward VI. It was used in beer making to give the mixture 'strength' and 'bite'.

CARAWAY This may be a plant native to Britain or perhaps it was introduced by the Romans. Both the roots and the seeds were eaten and were much used in seed cakes. It still grows wild in Britain and Europe.

CARDOON A member of the thistle family and in appearance not unlike a large head of celery. A vegetable once popular in Britain but now scarcely known.

CARP Mentioned in Richard II's time, also reintroduced in Henry VIII's reign. Izaak Walton, writing in 1653, gave some elaborate recipes for cooking carp.

CARROT At one time carrots grew wild with skirret and parsnips. They were not introduced as a garden vegetable into England until the sixteenth century. Ladies of Charles I's court used to wear the foliage as a decoration.

CAULIFLOWERS Brought into England from Cyprus in 1603.

CELERIAC Also called turnip-rooted celery, it was known in Britain in the eighteenth century but is almost unknown here today. It is grown in large quantities on the Continent.

CHAMPAGNE This was introduced into England during the seventeenth century, remained a rarity for about 100 years, then became popular.

CHEESE England imported Brie in 1278. The rich in medieval days knew a fairly wide variety of cheeses, but for most people there was soft and hard cheese. Cheshire is said to be the oldest English cheese, dating back to the twelfth century. Wensleydale, originally produced by Cistercian monks, was made of sheeps' milk until the seventeenth century.

Butter-making and work in the dairy.

CHERRIES Introduced to Rome by Lucullus in 70 B.C. and existed in England in 42 B.C. Pliny says the Romans brought them into England. They were mentioned in *The Forme of Cury*, and were 'cried' in the London streets in the fourteenth and fifteenth centuries as 'cherryes on the ryse' (on the twig). These were more likely to have been wild cherries for it was not until Tudor times that cherries began to be cultivated.

CHERVIL A delicate herb brought by the Romans into Britain. It was cultivated in Holborn in 1590 but not generally grown until 1726. It is not much grown today in Britain but it is important in France.

CHESTNUTS Another introduction of the Romans, and mentioned by Chaucer. In 1822 there was a tree at Fortworth, Gloucestershire, which had been there since 1150.

CHIVES A native plant to Britain and was called Cynes. They were probably not cultivated until the Middle Ages.

CHOCOLATE Although the Spaniards first brought this to Europe in 1520 it was not until the seventeenth century that the first chocolate house was opened in London. Chocolate appeared in tablet form in 1659. The introduction of chocolate (and coffee) created the need to import more sugar.

CHRISTMAS PUDDING See PLUM PORRIDGE.

CITRONS Imported in the time of Edward I (see Glossary).

COD Mentioned as early as the fourteenth century.

COFFEE Mentioned by Evelyn in 1636, it was introduced at Balliol College in 1641 by Mr Nathaniel Conopius, a Cretan. The first English coffee house was the Angel at Oxford in 1650. Coffee cost four to five guineas a pound at that time.

CRANBERRY A native of England which grew in the peaty bogs of Sussex, Cumberland, Norfolk and Lancashire.

CRAYFISH Noted in Henry VIII's time.

CRECY SOUP An English soup except for the name which is supposedly in memory of the great battle on August 26, 1346, where the English 'watered the carrots of Crecy with the best French blood'.

CREPE A type of pancake called crisp or cresp in Chaucer's time.

CUCUMBER Originally a Roman importation but it disappeared from the English scene. Cucumber was also another name for marrow. During the Wars of the Roses cucumbers (or marrows) were neglected but were finally rediscovered in the sixteenth century. They had a bad reputation and Evelyn, the diarist, considered them poisonous.

CURRANTS These once grew wild in Yorkshire, Durham, Westmorland and Tayside, but it is said they were introduced from the Continent. They got their name, which is misleading, because of their resemblance to the small grapes from Corinth, called currants. Henry Lyte, writing in 1578, calls them 'beyond the sea gooseberries'. They are related to gooseberries.

DAMSONS A plum from Damascus, brought into Britain by the returning Crusaders.

DANDELION A native plant used in salads and wine-making.

DATES Also brought to Britain by the Crusaders, and referred to in *The Forme of Cury*.

DILL William the Conqueror had a cook named Tezlin who made a white soup called *dillegrout*.

EELS An early favourite in Britain, especially in the monasteries.

ELDER A common wayside tree native to Britain and used in wine-making, tisanes, fritters etc., or as a flavouring.

ENDIVE This was also called succory or chicory and grew wild. True cultivation started about 1548.

FENNEL An ancient herb. In a fourteenth-century manuscript it is described as an 'erbe precows'.

FIGS Brought to Britain by the Crusaders and mentioned in *The Forme of Cury*. Both Edward I and Henry VIII are reputed to have planted fig trees. Fig trees grew against walls in Oxford about 1600.

FILBERTS Nuts of cultivated hazel, grown extensively in Britain since Queen Elizabeth I's time, but a Roman importation.

GARLIC Existed in medieval times, partially disappeared, was reintroduced to Britain in 1548 and was much employed.

GIN There were considerable imports of Dutch gin in the seventeenth century. It was cheap and soon English distillers brewed their own.

GINGER Used in Henry III's time, then neglected and reintroduced into Britain by the Dutch in 1566. Chaucer talks of gingerbread.

GINGERBREAD See page 45.

GOOSEBERRIES Brought from the Continent in the sixteenth century. King Henry VIII had gooseberries planted in his garden in 1516.

GRAPES These were grown in Britain from AD 10 and were mentioned by Bede; also they found their place in the *Domesday Book*. The Isles of Vines at Ely were planted by the Normans and the bishop received 3–4 tons of wine annually. Ely was famous for its grapes as late as 1653, but the suppression of the monasteries and the importation of cheap wines from the Continent caused a neglect of viniculture in Britain. It was not until much later that the English hot-house grapes became famous.

GREENGAGES Brought to England in the eighteenth century by a member of the Gage family from a French monastery garden where they were called Reine Claude. A variety of plum.

HADDOCK Recorded in the time of Edward I.

HAGGIS In Roman days and long after this there was a variety of boiled savoury pudding. Robert Burns in the eighteenth century called it 'Great Chieften of the Puddin' race'.

HERRINGS Scotland had the first known herring fishery in Europe. Yarmouth herrings were a staple Lenten food in the twelfth century. They were mentioned in literature soon after the Norman Conquest.

HOPS Introduced into England by Dutch gardeners in the early 1520s. Previously ground-ivy had been used for preserving beer.

HORSE-RADISH This grew wild in Britain before the Romans came. It was used medicinally, but was also known as a condiment.

HYSSOP A shrubby plant of ancient Mediterranean origin and mainly used medicinally.

KALEWORT See CABBAGE.

LAMPREY A scaleless fish of ancient renown. The most favoured were the eel lampreys. (See Glossary.)

LEEK A vegetable of such antiquity its origin is obscure. The Pharaohs grew it and probably the Romans brought it to Britain. The Welsh wear it as an emblem of their victory over the Saxons in the sixth century.

LEMONS Lemons probably arrived in Europe about the middle of the first century but possibly later. The Crusaders seem to have introduced lemons here. Attempts were made to cultivate lemons in this country in the reign of James I. They were 'cried' on the London streets at the turn of the sixteenth century.

LENTILS Imported into England in 1548.

LETTUCE It is not known when lettuces were introduced into Britain but in 1440 they were mentioned in John Gardner's *Feate of Gardening*. Thomas Cogan wrote 'lettuce is much used in the summer tyme, with vinegar, oyle and sugar and salt, and is formed to procure appetite for meate, and to temper the heate of the stomach and liver'.

LIQUORICE Popular since the time of Henry III.

MACKEREL The 'first mackerel in June' is mentioned between 1247–90.

MALMSLEY A popular fifteenth-century sweet wine, also called malmsey. (See Glossary.)

MARIGOLD Its petals were used in broths as well as medicinally. Marigolds were 'cried' in the streets of London, according to the *Roxburgh Ballads*.

MARJORAM Used since the earliest times but especially during the reign of Elizabeth I in broths, wafer cakes etc.

MARMALADE Mentioned about the end of the fifteenth century but referring usually to a preserve of quinces. Orange marmalade was first made in 1769.

MAYONNAISE It is interesting to note that Mary Queen of Scots is said to have invented this sauce.

MEAD and METHEGLIN Medieval drinks. (See Glossary.)

MEDLARS An old-fashioned little brown fruit the size of an apple with a firm flesh. Chaucer spoke of them.

MELONS Existed in Edward III's time, also planted in 1520. Melons, especially musk melons, grew in Britain in the seventeenth century.

MINT The Romans used mint and doubtless imported it into Britain. It became a favourite herb in the Middle Ages.

MULBERRIES Another Roman gift to us and mentioned in *The Forme of Cury*.

MUSTARD Possibly another Roman gift. Usually the seeds were ground in special little querns (such a quern is listed in an inventory of 1356 from a house in Cornhill) and mixed with must to make a sauce rather like mayonnaise. Later it was ground in Tewkesbury, Gloucestershire, a famous centre for mustard, made into balls and sent to other parts of the country. Shakespeare wrote: 'His wit is as thick as Tewkesbury mustard' (*Henry IV, Part II*). Mustard as we know it today was evolved in 1730 by a Mrs Clements of Durham. It won the approval of the royal family and became known as Durham Mustard.

NASTURTIUM Also known as Indian Cress and introduced into England about 1580. It came from Peru.

NECTARINE A type of peach introduced to England in 1524 and mentioned by John Parkinson in his important book on English gardening, *Paradisus Terrestris* (1629).

OLIVE OIL Used since the time of Henry III. Unsuccessful attempts to cultivate olives in England were made in 1570.

ONIONS These have been known since Roman times in Britain but they are older than recorded history.

ORANGES These originated in Asia and the first citrus fruits, including seven oranges, were brought by a Spanish ship to Britain in the fourteenth century. They were served at a royal banquet in 1399. They were 'cried' on the streets of London in the seventeenth century. Orange trees planted in tubs in the time of Charles I bore fruit and were taken indoors in winter. Queen Henrietta Maria had an orangery and an orange garden in Surrey.

OYSTERS Existed in England from at least 50 BC and were called 'natives'. See page 10.

PANCAKES Existed in England from medieval times. See CREPE.

PARSLEY Introduced into England in 1548.

PARSNIPS A native of Britain and cultivated since Roman times. Because of their sugar content, cakes and jams or conserves were made from them; also Irish beer. They were also dried and powdered for use as a sweetener. Originally known as pasternaks.

PEACHES Supposedly brought back by the Crusaders, and mentioned by Chaucer. In 1551 they were still rare but known in upper-class circles. They were cultivated in England in 1562. John Gerard, the herbalist, mentions four kinds of peaches.

PEACOCK These have been eaten since the earliest times in Greece and in Rome; but in Britain, when peacock feasts were fashionable among the nobles, much later. A brass on the floor of St Margaret's, King's Lynn, Norfolk, represents such a feast, dated 1364. They were served at tournaments, pageants etc., and were served up with extraordinary grandeur in a pastry case or 'coffin', with neck erect and tail expanded above the crust with beak and comb richly encrusted. They were carried into the dining-room on a gold or silver charger to a blast of trumpets and placed before the knight who had won the laurels of the day.

The peacock feast from St Margaret's, King's Lynn.

PEARS These are indigenous to England and were mentioned in *The Forme of Cury*. Warden pears originated at a Cistercian monastery in Bedfordshire (three warden pears were borne as the arms of the house). Pears were also imported in 1293. Pears in syrup were served at Henry IV's wedding feast, but it is said that pears and ale hastened the end of King John at Newark.

PEAS Introduced into England in Henry VIII's reign. Dried peas were eaten by sea-going people. Sugar peas were popular and rouncival peas were a delicacy in Tudor times and part of the staple vegetable diet.

PEPPER Imported into Britain since the eleventh century. The Company of Pepperers existed from this time and it was first mentioned as a guild in the time of Henry II. Later it became the Grocers and was incorporated in that name in 1345. Its members were mostly of Italian descent, from Lombardy, and settled in London thus giving Lombard Street its name.

PIKE The King's pike pond at Southwark kept the royal tables provided in Tudor and Stuart times.

PINEAPPLES Imported into England in 1664. Mentioned by Lord Bacon.

PLUMS Introduced by the Romans. There was a wild bullace or plum indigenous to England. Chaucer mentions plums, and Lord Cromwell presented several kinds to Henry VIII in 1520.

PLUM PORRIDGE This can be traced to Teutonic days and was originally a porridge containing raisins, currants and prunes but is nevertheless the predecessor to plum or plumb pudding, and our present Christmas pudding.

POMEGRANATE An Old Testament fruit imported into England in the reign of Edward I, and mentioned in *The Forme of Cury*. Pomegranates were grown in boxes in Wimbledon in 1649 but had been cultivated in England since 1548.

PORPOISES These were also called sea-swine and were considered a delicacy in the thirteenth century. Richard II served them and they were a first course at the Coronation banquet of Henry VII. They were boiled, made into 'puddings' and pasties as late as Queen Elizabeth I's day, but went out of fashion about 1575. See page 19.

POTATOES Originally introduced by Sir Francis Drake or Sir John Hawkins to Ireland in 1565, and Sir Walter Raleigh brought them to England. Although not known in England till 1588, they were familiar by 1633 but used as a 'delicate' dish, not becoming a common food for about another 150 years. Shakespeare causes Falstaff to exclaim in the *Merry Wives of Windsor*, 'let the sky rain potatoes'. Despite considerable interest, potatoes remained for a long time a curiosity.

PRUNES Mentioned in *The Forme of Cury*.

PUDDINGS Sweet puddings became popular in Britain during the mid-seventeenth century when sugar became cheaper. A French visitor, M. Misson, wrote enthusiastically: 'Blessed be he that invented pudding, for it is a manna that hits the palates of all sortes of people.'

PUMPKINS These were planted in Britain during the sixteenth century but were only eaten by the lower classes. They were known better as 'pompian' and were made into 'pies'. A hole was cut into the side of the fruit, the seeds and filament removed, and the hollow filled with apples and spicery. The hole was closed and the pumpkins baked. This dish was taken to the United States of America and is a forerunner of the Thanksgiving Pumpkin Pie.

QUINCES Introduced originally by the Romans and one of the earliest fruits mentioned in *The Forme of Cury*, also by Chaucer but as 'coynes'. Quinces were reintroduced to England via Austria in the sixteenth century.

RADISH Among the oldest known vegetables, it was common to the Greeks and Romans and was popular in Britain by the Middle Ages.

RAISINS Mentioned as early as the reign of Edward I, and in *The Forme of Cury* recipes including raisins are given.

RASPBERRY One of the oldest fruits and cultivated in Britain since 1548. Cakes were made from raspberries.

RHUBARB Introduced into Britain by Andrew Boorde in 1573, who sent rhubarb to Thomas Cromwell explaining 'the whiche comes owte of Barbery' (he meant, curiously, the Volga region of Russia). It was not marketed in England until 1810 as it was viewed with considerable suspicion.

RICE Imported into England in the time of Henry III.

ROSEMARY Introduced into Britain by the Romans.

ROSES These were among the flowers used in old-time cooking. Roses were preserved, candied etc.

RUE Another Roman introduction.

SAFFRON Introduced into England during Edward III's reign.

SAGE It is uncertain when sage was first used in European cooking. The Romans used it in medicine but not in cooking.

SAGO Imported into England from 1580, a product of the sago tree with long-keeping qualities.

SALMON Mentioned specifically during the reign of Edward I. It was salted and pickled and considered a stately fish.

SALT An early discovery in culinary development. There was already a Salters Company, chartered in 1394, as a result of the large trade in salt.

SALT-FISH First mentioned in the time of Edward I. Home-salted fish was considered superior to foreign fish in Elizabethan times, and there was a large salt-fish trade between Britain and Norway.

SAUCES Piquant sauces were popular in medieval days and made of expensive condiments and rare spices. A statute of Edward III prohibited the making of sauces unless at a moderate cost. Sauce makers are mentioned in a roll of the citizens of York at the beginning of the fourteenth century.

Boar's head served at a convivial supper of Canterbury pilgrims.

SAVORY A herb cultivated in 1562 and used in cakes, puddings, sausages etc.

SKIRRETS A water parsnip. Skirret pie was a popular dish in early days.

SOUP Recorded as early as Anglo-Saxon days.

SPICES The spice trade is one of the oldest. The Pepperers were already organized by the eleventh century.

SPINACH As early as the fifteenth century this was listed as a garden plant and used in sweet dishes. Originally it was called 'Spanish vegetable' as it was thought to have come from Spain.

STRAWBERRIES The wood or wild strawberry is indigenous. Garden strawberries were imported from Virginia in 1629.

STURGEON Mentioned as a royal fish as early as Edward I's time and more abundant then than today.

SUGAR Imported to Britain from India and Arabia in 1535, it was first planted in Rhodes and Malta, then Sicily, Madeira, Canary Islands and the West Indies (Jamaica) in 1660. First it was used as a medicine, then as a substitute for honey, and eaten with meat to correct the putrescence. It was originally introduced after the Crusades and was very expensive but became cheaper after the discovery of America. In 1471 a Venetian discovered how to purify brown sugar. Sugar loaves were mentioned in the fifteenth century. Sugar was refined in England before 1596, and made into loaves at Bristol in 1654. The sugar grown in Sicily in the thirteenth century may have been white. Between 1700 and 1800 English sugar consumption rose by fifteen times, partly because of the huge consumption of chocolate and coffee.

SWAN A royal and expensive bird. Richard II had 50 of them served at one of his banquets. The larger the swan, the more they were appreciated.

TANSY Tansy creams and Easter cakes were once a favourite, and tansy was used as a corrective after too much fish. (See Glossary.)

TEA This was first brought to Europe in the seventeenth century and by the middle of the following century it was the principal beverage in England.

TOMATOES These were brought by the Spaniards to Europe in the fifteenth century. Sir Walter Raleigh presented Queen Elizabeth I with tomato plants as a decoration. Such was the prejudice against eating them that they did not become popular until the nineteenth century. In France they were eaten in the seventeenth century.

TURKEY This name was first given to the guinea fowl. The turkey we now know was discovered in Mexico and brought by the Spaniards to Europe in 1530. But their history is not clear and when Shakespeare spoke of turkeys he doubtless meant guinea fowl. The confusion seems to have lasted until well into the seventeenth century.

TURNIPS Much used by the poor before potatoes became popular; eaten baked or roasted in ashes in Henry VIII's time. Turnip tops were used as saladings, but widespread cultivation was not begun until the seventeenth century.

WALNUTS Walnuts have been grown in Britain since earliest times, introduced by the Romans. They are indigenous to Persia but were carried on English trading ships and thus earned the name English walnuts.

WHALE This was eaten by the Saxons and continued to be eaten until the fifteenth century. Whales found on the British coasts were the perquisites of the monarch until recently; those found on the banks of the Thames, of the Lord Mayor of London. The Countess of Leicester in the thirteenth century served whale. The Normans boiled it and served it with peas. Connoisseurs ate the tail or the tongue. Whale fisheries are of ancient origin.

WHEAT The Saxons ate bread of fine wheaten flour.

WHISKY Called usquebaugh in the seventeenth century.

WHITEBAIT These small fish used to swarm the Thames and were formerly used as bait, hence the name.

WINES Wines were first imported into Britain by the Romans and later were made in Britain. By the middle of the twelfth century large areas of the country were covered by vineyards. The wine trade with France began in 1154 with the marriage of Henry II to Eleanor of Aquitaine.

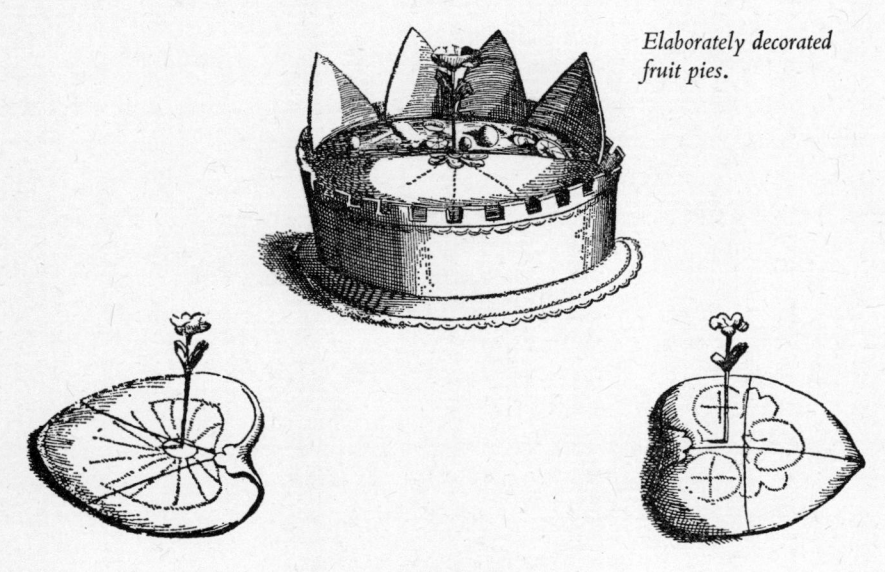

Elaborately decorated fruit pies.

Table Manners

That 'manners maketh the man' was obviously not a practised medieval precept. Anglo-Danish manners were deplorably crude. Diners quarrelled among themselves at table, grabbed food in an unseemly manner, smacked their lips 'loud and clear', gurgled and burped, shovelled their food into their mouths until their cheeks filled out like the sacks of bagpipes, or, as one chronicler put it, 'until men say he has a mouth like an ape'.

Not a pretty picture! Nor is the illustration of what happened at the dining table given in Alexander Barclay's *Eclogues* (1570):

> *If the fish be pleasaunt, eyther fleshe or fishe,*
> *Ten handes at once swarme in the dishe:*
> *And if it be fleshe, ten knives shall thou see*
> *Mangling the flesh, and in the platter flee:*
> *To put there thy hands is perill without fayle,*
> *Without a gauntlet or els a glove of mayle.*

Eating was a thoroughly sloppy business. The diner having literally grabbed a choice piece of food from a dish, brimming with gravy, and dipped it into a bowl of sauce, the dripping gobbit of flesh was carried over the table cloth to the mouth. If it were a chunk of meat still on the bone, the bone was picked clean and then thrown to the dogs round the table.

Such behaviour, disgusting to many, brought about a spate of books on good manners at the table. In the *Boke of Curtasye* (*circa* 1430) the author is explicit in his advice and points an admonishing finger at the reader. He tells him to clean his nails before coming to the table. Don't drink with food in your mouth as you may get choked or killed by its stopping your wind. Don't stroke the dog or cat while at table. Don't dirty the tablecloth with your knife. Don't blow on your food or put your knife in your mouth, or wipe your teeth or eyes on the tablecloth. Don't lean your elbows on the table, or dip your thumb in your drink, or your food in the salt-cellar. Finally, when the diner washes his hands (and hopefully his face) he should not spit in the basin, and in the presence of a man of God, he should take special heed of where he spits.

Obviously such a general crudeness of manners continued well into the Elizabethan era, for we have *The Boke of Nurture, or Schoole of Good Manners:* compyled by Hugh Rhodes of the Kinges Chappell (born and bred in Devonshyre) imprinted at London, 1577, which tells its readers all this and more. This little book is charmingly illustrated with woodcuts, the most attractive of these being one on the Lord's Prayer.

This is probably the most entertaining and worthwhile book on table manners of the sixteenth century and could be described as a handbook of table etiquette.

The following don'ts give us a pretty good idea of how people behaved at that time.

> *Before you sit down to meals, see that your knife is clean and sharp, your hands clean and your nails pared.*
>
> *Don't put too much bread in the soup. Don't crumble it into the dish you share, but cut it in case you have sweaty hands. After your soup, wipe your spoon clean and lay it down.*
>
> *Fill not thy spone too full, lest thou lose somewhat by the way.*
>
> *Dip not thy meat in the salt seller, but take it with a knife.*
>
> *Furnish no bones with thy teeth, for that is unseemly.*
>
> *Help to serve strangers with dainties, and anyone who cannot get close to the dish.*

A monk succumbs to the sin of gluttony.

Eate softly and drink mannerly, beware ye do not quaffe. Scratch not thy head or finger when thou art at meate.

Pick not thy teeth with thy knife, nor finger ende, but with a stick or some cleane thing, then do ye not offend.

Pick not thy hands, nor play with thy knife, Keepe still foot and hand, at meat time begin ye no stryfe (argument).

Wipe they mouth when thou shalt drink Ale or wine, On thy napkin onely, and see all things be cleane, Blow not your nose in the napkin, where ye wipe your hand.

With your napkin ye may oft wipe your mouth clean, Some thing thereon will cleave, that every man may it see.

Fill not thy mouth to full, least thou must nedes speake, Nor blow not out they crums, when thou doest eat. Role not thy meat in thy mouth that every man may it see.

Don't drink too much.

Don't leave too many morsels in your trencher but push them into the voyder.

Don't blow on the soup, as your breath may not be holesome. Don't throw the bones under the table. Don't stretch and lean on the table. Don't carve the table with your knife.

After grace, say to your fellow-diners 'Much good do it ye'.

Children were not forgotten in the general condemnation of table manners, and the *Lytel Report on How Young People Should Behave*, published *circa* 1475, has some decided advice, much of which applies today.

Cut your bread, don't break it.

Lay a clean trencher before you, and eat your broth with a spoon, don't sup it up.

Don't hang your head over your dish, or pick your nose, teeth or nails . . . or put your knife in your mouth.

Take every dish that is brought to you, and when once your plate is taken away don't ask for it again.

Have a clean trencher and knife for your cheese, and eat properly. When the meal is over, clean your knives and put these in their places, keep your seate till you have washed.

The *Young Children's Book* admonishes:

Touch nothing until you are fully helped.

Don't break your bread in two or put it in your pocket.

Nor put your fingers in the dish.

Don't grin or talk too much or spill your food.

Drink behind no man's back.

Don't rush at the cheese.

Don't wipe your knife on the cloth and don't wipe your nose at the table.

Finally, three decisive don'ts (it would seem in those days no one was afraid of saying don't to the young),

Don't butter your bread with your thumb

Don't eat bread picked off the floor

Don't poke your fingers into eggs

All of which would seem to prove that our ancestors were indeed sloppy eaters.

A meal in a Jacobean household. Children were expected to show good table manners as much as their elders and betters.

Concerning Waffles and Wafers

What today is called a wafer is a thin and light type of biscuit that is served with some sweet puddings, with ice-cream and sweet wines, also often in France with champagne. A waffle is now made from a light spongy mixture and baked on top of the stove in a waffle iron, and is generally associated by most people in Britain with American cooking.

Wafers and waffles have been part of European culinary history for centuries. They are mentioned in *Piers Plowman*, also by Chaucer in his *Canterbury Tales*, with some affectionate reverence. There is little doubt that our ancestors were extremely fond of these 'little compositions of flour, sugar and eggs', and that they were a popular treat for noble and peasant alike.

There was an office at the Royal Court styled The Wafery, the officers of which were solely employed in making wafers for the royal palace. (According to the Oxford English Dictionary, a wafery is a room in which wafers were made.) Cardinal Wolsey was apparently so fond of wafers that he employed two waferers in his private wafery. These early wafers were not as thin as our present-day kind, but much more like today's waffles.

Wafers or waffles – it is hard to separate them – were hawked in the streets, sold at booths in fairs, and close to church and cathedral doors during important religious festivals. The waffle or wafer seller would place his stall as near to the church as allowed, set up his charcoal fire, make his batter and then bake his waffles. He hardly needed to cry his wares since the appetizing and tantalizing aroma of the freshly baked sweet batter drew the pennies from his customers.

Wafers are listed in the items for an archbishop's feast held as early as 1295. It was also a traditional custom to present the royal couple with spiced wafers at a royal banquet, to take with the hippocras. They were given as a mid-Lenten treat on the fourth Sunday in Lent, mainly to young female servants to present to their mothers. This Sunday became known as Wafering Sunday or Refreshment Sunday, also Mothering Sunday. As late as the eighteenth century there was still an official wafer maker (waferer) at Leckford in Hampshire.

Although many of the early wafer irons have turned up in old farmhouses, the early recipe manuscripts do not give wafer recipes. The earliest English recipe appears to be that written by Sir Hugh Plat in 1609:

To make Wafers
To make the best *Wafers*, take the finest wheat-flower you can get, and mixe it with creame, the yelkes of eggs, rosewater, sugar, and cinnamon til it be a little thicker than Pan-cake batter; and then warming your wafer-yrons on a charcoale fire, annoint them first with sweete butter, and then lay on your batter and presse it, and bake it white or brown at your pleasure.

A recipe taken from Gervase Markham's *Country Contentments*, 1623, runs:

To make Wafers
Take a pinte of flowre, put it into a little creame with two yolkes of egges and a little rosewater, with a little searced Sinamon and Sugar, worke them altogether and bake the paste upon hote Irons.

It would seem that Markham favoured the firmer French form of batter than the usual loose English type. Sweet butter is our unsalted butter; in America it is still so called.

Those early wafer irons are today's museum pieces. The work of craftsmen, they date back to the Middle Ages. In the Victoria and Albert collection there are some fine Italian irons which an expert considered were all made by one family in Perugia. This family, according to Dr W. L. Fildeburgh, were the sole makers of wafer irons in Italy until some time in the sixteenth century. Many of the Italian wafer irons show the arms of ancient Venetian families, while others have mottoes and sporting scenes. Some of the irons were as small as 4 inches in diameter, and others were twice that size.

In England the irons were simpler in design but seldom were there ever two alike. Like the Italian irons, they were stamped with sporting or hunting scenes, landscapes or flowers. Some had religious motifs, like the church wafer irons. Others had quotations, some rather moral, for example:

'Happy is he who measures all his steps and who beholds the end of his labour.'

'Wafers with sweet wine are perfect, but drink often and they will disappear quickly.'

'When irons are hot, then hasten, for the time flies, and always pursues thee.'

'Eat the wafers and then drink, that you may take the bear with a net.' (i.e. you will be fit for anything.)

'To me that makes the wafers it is a duty to give me to drink whatever I wish.'

'Wafers are good at breakfast especially while they are hot.'

And so on.

Wafering irons, also known as waffle irons or tongs, consisted of two flat discs instead of long jaws; these were incised (embossed) with a different pattern on the inside surface of each, and there were two handles about 2½ feet long. One handle usually ended in a knob, and the other in a ring which slipped over the knob of the other handle so that the jaws or discs could be held tightly with the batter between them.

The irons consisted of two main types, one usually circular, to make the very thin wafers, one imagines somewhat like the ice-cream wafers of today. The other was rectangular, obviously to make a thicker wafer, more similar to the present-day American waffle.

The batter used by the English on the whole was thin – somewhat thicker than a pancake batter – and was dropped on the iron in spoonfuls. But the French batter was quite thick and firm, and was rolled out before being put on the wafer iron.

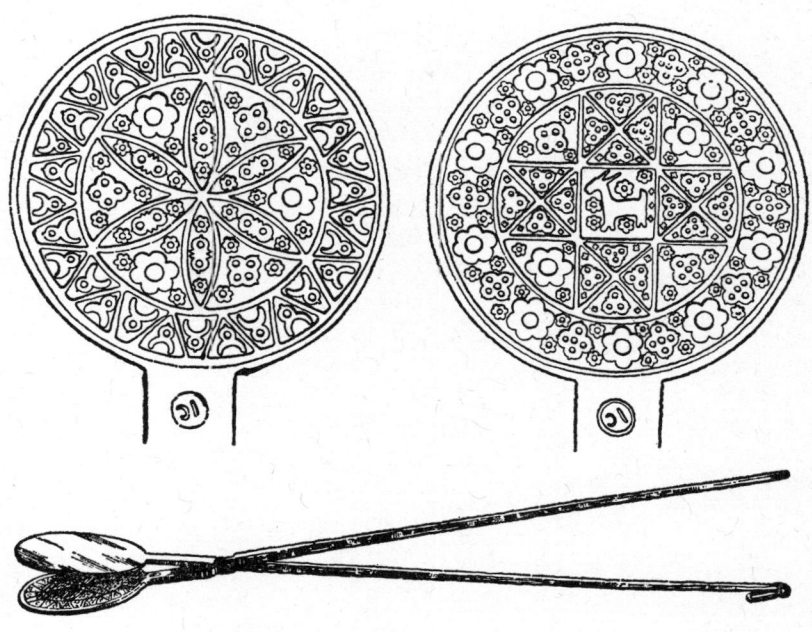

Patterned wafering irons of the sixteenth century.

Gingerbread

One imagines there was always gingerbread. It was reputedly invented by a Greek baker from Rhodes, and is said to be the oldest cake-bread in the world. It was not a cake as we know it today but a solid slab of honey, flour and spices etc. – but (certainly in England) not including ginger. This came later although not as late as treacle, which was introduced into England in 1694.

England knew gingerbread (see glossary for other spellings) in early days. Chaucer wrote: 'They sette hym Roiall spicery and gyngebread'. And Shakespeare gave us in *Love's Labour's Lost*: 'An had I one penny in the world thou shoulds't have it to buy gingerbread.' The author of *The Forme of Cury* gave us a gingerbread recipe, as did other early cookery authorities, including the amiable Gervase Markham. In *Bartholomew Fair*, one of Ben Jonson's characters is a gingerbread woman. Gingerbread was sold in the streets to the cry of 'Come, buy my spice-gingerbread, smoking hot! hot!' At St Bartholomew's Fair in the fourteenth century gingerbreads were sold for 20 a penny, and called 'fairings'.

It was not a humble cake – on the contrary, it was welcomed by noble and peasant alike. It was accepted both as an article of food and as a popular gift, much as today we might offer a box of chocolates. It was given as a present at births, weddings and funerals, designs being different for each occasion. There were gingerbreads of 'honour' which were often presented at court; there were gingerbreads given by patrons to their workmen, and *vice versa*; the young gave them to the old as a sign of respect and even humility. Some of these presentation gingerbreads made to order were fantastic, over a yard wide and weighing up to 150 lb. or more.

Originally gingerbread in England was made with grated bread, moistened with wine or honey and coloured either yellow with saffron or more often with saunders (red), and flavoured with various spices. The mixture was pressed into a mould, the top neatly levelled off with a palette knife and the mixture baked in a warm oven.

As soon as the gingerbread came out of the oven it was gilded with gold or Dutch leaf, applied while the gingerbread was still hot or, as the old recipe put it, 'An' if you will hyn gilt doe it now.' The gingerbread could, of course, be served at once but it was often put into a box and stored away for up to a year.

Gingerbread moulds were made in all sorts of fanciful shapes and old illustrations provide some delightful instances of carved wooden gingerbread and marchpane (see Glossary) moulds. It is not always easy to decide which moulds were for gingerbread and which for marchpane, but it is more likely that the more elaborate moulds were for the latter as the soft mixture was pressed into them while still warm (see page 102) and thus could take the splendid imprint. The moulds, kept by the bakers, had been in families for generations. On the whole, the English moulds tended to be less elaborate than those used on the Continent, although it is more likely that gingerbread moulds came to England in Elizabethan times as a result of Italian influence. Before the use of moulds, bakers used rolling pins heavily embossed with patterns which had been in use since the days of Henry VII.

Gingerbread baked in moulds continued to be fashionable both as a delicious bread-cake and as a gift. Georgian hostesses had gingerbread moulds made with their coats of arms, or sporting scenes or other similar decorations. Boxwood, beech, walnut and pear wood were all used to make the moulds, which were square-shaped, round, and even heart-shaped. In the Balkans and other parts of Europe, gingerbreads are still made in heart-shaped moulds, heavily iced, and sold at the country fairs and during festivals.

There were cakes known as 'book-gingerbread' which were stamped with the letters of the alphabet – a very clever idea to teach children to read. As Matthew Prior wrote in 1721:

> *To master John the English Maid*
> *A Horn-book gives of Ginger-bread;*
> *And that the Child may learn the better,*
> *As he can name he eats the letter.*

Such gingerbread was sold at the country fairs, and bought at a halfpenny a slice until as late as the end of the last century.

Apart from moulds and rolling pins, gingerbreads were also baked in a type of old waffle iron.

Table Equipment

Spoons

The word spoon is said to have come from O.E. *spon*, a chip. Neolithic finds show clumsily carved spoons of wood, metal and bronze. The Romans had elegant spoons made of silver, some of which were copied from the shape of shells, which probably first suggested spoons to man; others had a long narrow stem with a painted end to extract snails from their shells. There were egg spoons with a round bowl and others with more pointed bowls, possibly for scooping out condiments. Although no one is sure when the first metal spoons were made, there are references to gold spoons in the Old Testament, and many indications that metal work had reached a high degree of craftsmanship by that time.

Silver spoons were in common use in the houses of the rich by the thirteenth century, but lesser folk were still content with spoons made of horn, wood or pewter. Those early spoons were often somewhat quaint in design: circular, elliptical, egg-shaped, fig-shaped – some even resembled the outline of a modern tennis racket. Many of the pewter spoons were copied from patterns used by the silversmiths, but they were generally large, of almost wooden spoon dimensions. The so-called fork-spoon was seen in the sixteenth century, a spoon sawn into long teeth in an attempt to unite the purposes of both. There were also spoons with long handles shaped like marrow scoops. The spoon was gradually adapted, and increasingly used to scoop up liquids, rather than pick up food.

Some interesting spoons were made in Tudor days, with handles six or seven inches long, a large bowl and a narrow stem terminating in a figure or an object on top called a knop. One popular knop was the figure of the Virgin Mary; these were called Maidenhead spoons. Of the other religious knops the so-called Apostle spoons were the most sought after. They were usually made by the silversmiths in sets of thirteen, one master spoon with the figure of Christ, his hand raised in blessing, and twelve minor spoons each with the figure of an apostle and his symbol, like St Peter with the key. There were also sets of the four Evangelists, and from time to time a single spoon would be made. Typical knops of a non-religious nature would be a bunch of grapes, a strawberry, or a 'lion-sejant' and the old man of the woods or the 'woodwose' complete with club. There were also 'double horn-headed' knops comprising a woman's head and headdress.

The custom of sponsors giving godchildren silver spoons, in particular Apostle spoons, as a christening present, originated in Tudor times. Lucky the child with a rich godparent, for he would receive a complete set of spoons. Somewhat poorer sponsors gave a set of the Evangelists, while the poor contented themselves with a single spoon, not always silver, but of wood or pewter. The really old pewter spoon is rare since pewter is not lasting and wears down with time – ironically, the humbler pewter spoon is often more highly valued than the silver one in consequence.

Among the most interesting spoons, meant not as table ware but as a gift of love, is the Welsh love spoon. It was the custom in Wales for an intending and serious lover to present the object of his affections with an ornamental wooden spoon, of his own carving. If accepted, this was placed on the chimney piece, and the courtship was officially acknowledged. This habit was very prevalent in Wales, and E. H. Pinto wrote that the Welsh love spoon 'was so universally a pre-courting question in wood, that the word "spooning" has passed into the English language'. As all these spoons were individually carved, the design taking shape as the lover worked, they were seldom, if ever, duplicated. (The Museum of Welsh Antiquities at the University College of North Wales has a fine collection of love spoons.)

Forks

Our ancestors must have believed firmly in the adage 'fingers before forks', for great was their reluctance to use forks. They were definitely in existence in the seventeenth century, yet we read that Queen Anne constantly ate with her fingers.

Forks of a kind were known in England at the time of William the Conqueror. In a list of effects of Edward I, taken after his death in 1307, there appears: 'six forks, one gold fork.' A small fork was known at the English Court in the Middle Ages. This was a small silver dessert fork of the type of which Piers Gaveston, a favourite of Edward II, owned three, '*pour manger les poires*'. Henry VII paid Master (or Mistress) Brent, silversmith, twelve shillings for a fork weighing three ounces. But forks continued as decorative luxuries until 1608. Perhaps the oldest known English fork, a two-pronged one made for the Earl of Rutland in 1632, is in the Victoria and Albert Museum.

Forks of various types, usually crude and simple, were used in early kitchens but seldom on the table. Sometimes a fork was included in a *nef* (see page 52). There was a type of fork with two small tines or prongs at one end of the stem and a spoon bowl at the other. Such forks were referred to as a 'spone with a suckette fork uppon one stele'. These were used for eating 'suckets' which were sweetmeals or preserves in syrup.

It was Thomas Coryat (sometimes spelt Coryate and Coryatt), who pioneered the use of forks in England. But all he got for his pains was laughter and derision. He had returned from one of his long walking tours in Europe which included a stay in Italy and France, and in 1611 he wrote an account of his journey calling it *Coryat's Crudities, hastily gobbled up in five Months' Travel*. He championed the use of forks.

'The Italian and also most strangers that are commorant in Italy, doe alwaies at their meales use a little forke when they cut their meate. For while with their knife which they hold in one hand they cut the meate out of the dish, they fasten their forke which they hold in their other hand upon the same dish, so that whatsoever he be that sitting in the company of any others at meale, should unadvisedly touch the dish of meate with his fingers from which all at the table doe cut, he will give occasion of offence unto the company, as having transgressed the lawes of good manners, in so much that for his error he shall be at the least brow-beaten, if not reprehended in wordes. This forme of feeding I understand is generally used in all places of Italy, their forkes being for the most part made of yron or steele, and some of silver, but those are used only by Gentlemen. The reason of this their curiosity is, because the Italian cannot by any means indure to have his dish touched with fingers, seeing all men's fingers are not alike cleane.'

Thomas Coryat put his plan of introducing the useful fork into action but instead of finding favour, even among the gallants of his day, he was considered affected, and they called him Furcifer, a nickname which stayed with him. It was a word originally applied to a defaulting slave who as a punishment had to walk through the streets with a fork-like gallows round his neck. The word had come to mean a rogue or villain. Poor Thomas! He was even denounced from the pulpit on the ground that it was impious to say that one of God's creatures was not fit to touch a dish with his fingers.

But the fork won through, though but slowly. In 1652 we read of 'the use of forks which is by some of our spruce gallants taken up of the later'. The author of *The Ingenuous Gentlewoman's Delightful Companion* (1653) wrote: 'it will be comely and decent to use a fork'. And by the end of the reign of Charles II, forks were seen on most well-appointed tables.

We do not find truly graceful forks until the reign of Queen Anne, when the three-tined fork with the so-called wavy end came into fashion. By the time of George II forks were larger, and a distinction was made between table and dessert forks. By the second half of the eighteenth century, heavy four-tined forks had appeared – but this is after our chosen period.

Knives

Man can manage without forks but not without knives. Even prehistoric man knew the value of a sharp edge and fashioned for himself flints to be held by the hand or to be mounted in a support. When iron replaced bronze as the established metal for knives, it was also realized that properly tempered wrought-iron could be made strong enough for a sword blade as well as for a knife. By the Middle Ages blades from the steel craftsmen of Toledo and Damascus were famed for their quality.

Originally there was little difference, if any, between a carving or hunting knife and the knife used at the table. Most men carried a kind of clasp knife in their belt or the pocket of their girdles, which they used at table. Early Saxon knives had razor-sharp edges and other early knives had a projection at the end to enable the user to pick up gobbits of meat and other titbits.

Knives then came in pairs, one for cutting meat, the other for bread, and they were carried in a special sheath attached to the wearer's belt. In the sixteenth and seventeenth centuries a knife called a *presentoir*, or serving knife, came into fashion. It was shaped rather like a spatula, the top end of the knife being much wider than the haft end. These knives were for lifting food from the main dish to the platter.

Changing fashions and habits brought a change in the shape of the knife. Still the blades were long, but the pointed end, so useful at table as a spear, disappeared. The tops were snapped off and they became almost square. In the seventeenth century the knife with the now-familiar rounded end came into use. Cardinal Richelieu, it is said, was so disgusted at the unappetizing picture of Chancellor Segieur busily picking his teeth with his knife after a meal, that he ordered his steward to round off the ends of all household knives. Such was the Cardinal's influence that soon everyone was using rounded-off knives, and by 1669 a decree was issued in France that all knives were to be made with rounded tops and that no one, however exalted, was to send pointed knives to the cutler to be sharpened.

It is not quite certain when knives were made specifically for the table. In the Bayeux Tapestry we see the table set with knives; also, Chaucer mentions table knives. Even when sets of knives began to appear in rich households, it was still customary for a gentleman to carry his own cutlery with him when he dined out. As late as the seventeenth century it was traditional to present to a bridal couple a pair of knives. These were as richly ornamented as the donor could afford, with silver handles bearing Biblical quotations.

The greater use of knives led to almost mass production, and the consequent lowering in their quality. Even so, fine workmanship was still much

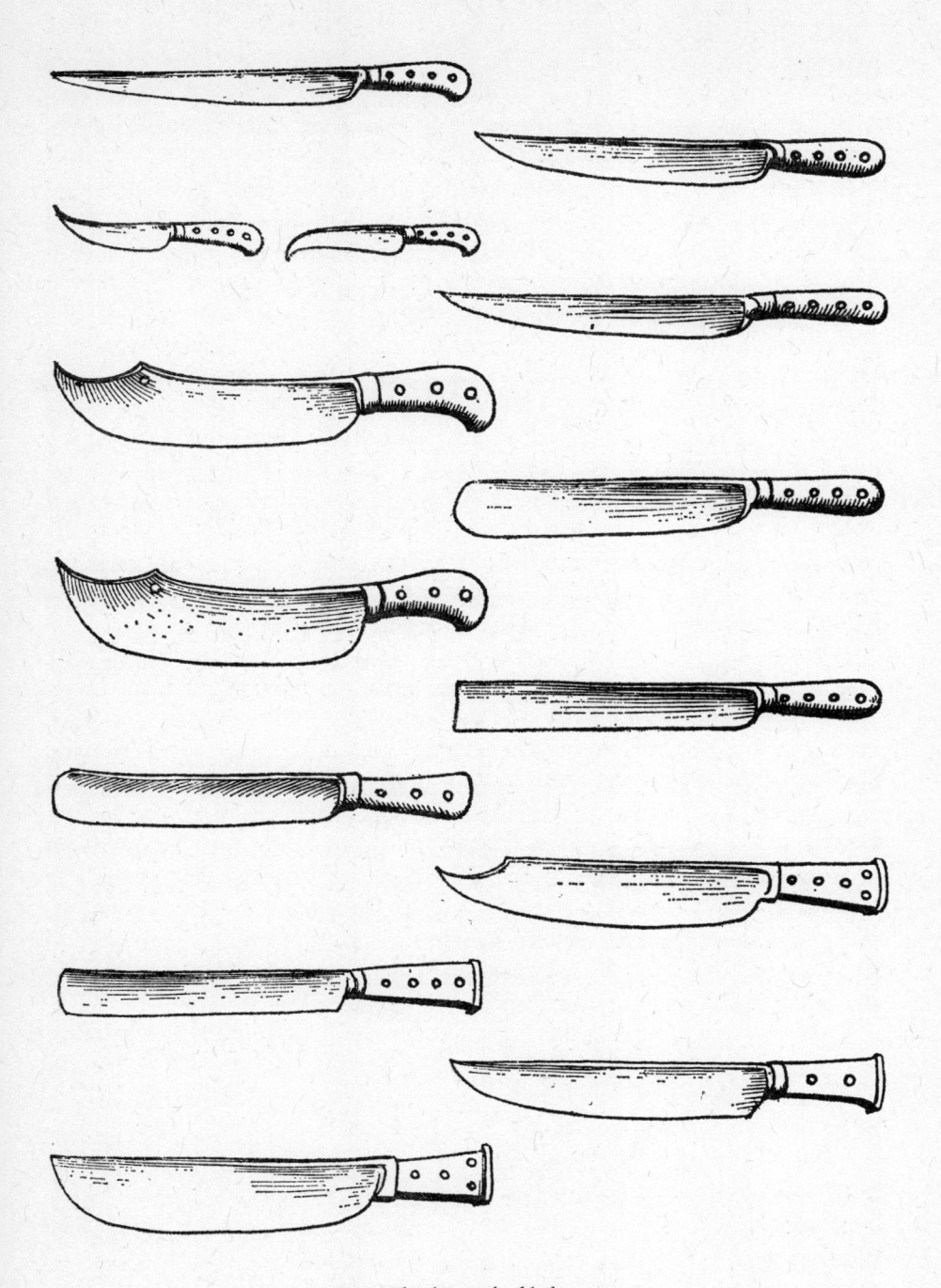

Various kitchen and table knives.

appreciated at the English Court. When Henry VIII died he left a case of knives garnished with precious stones, such as rubies, emeralds, amethysts. In an inventory of Queen Elizabeth I's effects no less than thirty-four cases of knives were listed.

Oddly enough, not all these knives were made in England. Many were imported from Flanders and other places. Not until the seventeenth century did English cutlers bother to introduce their own markings, and by this time there had developed what could be called the English shape.

An interesting custom was the use of hafting knives, or special knives used during the different religious festivals of the year. This was a convention which started probably in the fourteenth century, and persisted right through to the seventeenth, obviously only for the rich. It consisted of having various sets of knives with differently coloured handles for different occasions: for example, during Lent, black-handled knives were used, at Eastertide, white-handled knives, while at Whitsun, the handles were chequered black and white.

Knife handles were fashioned from all kinds of materials: silver, horn, ivory, glass, rock crystal, agate, wood and even china. Later, ivory-green handles were produced to imitate the much more expensive malachite.

The life of the knife blade was short, for constant cleaning and grinding to keep the edges sharp wore the blade away. However, it is still possible to see some rare specimens of early knives in museums.

Towards the end of the seventeenth century the scimitar knife was introduced, and this became the basis of all knives throughout the Georgian era, and was then abandoned in favour of the straight-bladed knife much like those of today. It was finely wrought in steel and the curve of the blade matched the curve of the handle, the then fashionable pistol-butt shape. Early models of this form of knife were made in solid silver, but later less heavy and expensive though more fashionable metals were used. In the same period, dessert knives and forks became fashionable; however, it was not until 1820 that the first steel edge was given to a silver blade.

Nef

This was an elaborate casket or container, usually in the form of a ship, raised on a stand. It was used in the late Middle Ages and took precedence over the great salt. It contained the lord's napkin, spoon, knife, spices and seasonings, his drinking vessel and a toothpick. Also it frequently contained a piece of narwhal, called an 'essay'. This, when mixed with wine, had properties which detected poison if present. The nef could be locked. It was brought to the table with some ceremony and laid in front of the prince or nobleman who owned it.

This important piece of ware, which also had ecclesiastical connections, was reserved for the tables of kings and noblemen, and some of them were extremely elaborate. Charles V of France, according to an inventory, owned five enamelled gold nefs and twenty-five silver ones. Apart from those which resembled a full-scale model of a sailing ship, there were others of different shapes. In 1392 a nef on wheels was recorded as being in the Papal collection.

In the sixteenth century ornaments, jugs and cups were made in this form, especially in Switzerland and Germany. Many of them were highly ornamental yet accurate models of ships, often richly enamelled and even 'crewed' with the tiny figures of sailors. Their shape is said to have originated in the thirteenth century when Queen Margaret, wife of Louis IX, dedicated a silver model of a fully-rigged ship to St Nicholas in thanksgiving after she and her three children had survived a severe storm off Cyprus when they were returning from Palestine to France, in 1254.

Salt-Cellars

Why salt-cellars? When Wynkyn de Worde wrote his meticulously detailed instructions on good manners and the setting of the table, he had this to say on the positioning of the salt: 'Set your salt on the ryght side where your soverayne shall sit', and 'at every end of ye table set a salte saller', thereby differentiating between the Salt and the smaller salts. At the same time he gave to the English language one of those odd quirks of corruption which have become part of it. This 'saller' or as we write today, cellar, was the old English spelling of an equally old French word *salière* or salt-box. Therefore, our prefix salt is superfluous, *saller* meant salt-box.

Salt-cellars were regarded with some esteem if not with a kind of reverence. It had long been known that salt was important to the health and vigour of man; and salt-mining was an old and often much-feared industry. The Greeks had consecrated salt to the gods, and the Laws of Moses declared it an emblem of purity, perfection and perpetuity. It is easy therefore to understand why, over the centuries, there were several curious customs concerning salt, the best known being that it is unlucky to spill it.

The salt-cellars of de Worde's day are what were later called trencher salts. Few of them have survived time and the melting pot. Many of these were massive and came in different shapes, some round, others rectangular or *quatrefoil*. It was an important piece of table equipment so perhaps we should not be surprised to learn that Edward III had salts enamelled with baboons and little birds, or that an Earl of March, in 1308, left to his son and daughter each a salt in the shape of a dog. There were those shaped like ships, and there was one (at least) in the shape of a chariot with four wheels, probably for the convenience of passing salt down the table.

In the Middle Ages the master sat in the middle of the table with the salt (also called salt-vat or salt-foot) in front of him, but just slightly to the right, where the chief guest sat. Thus the salt was as near to the guest as to the host. Other guests were seated to the right or left as befitted their rank. Later, it was the custom for the master to sit at the end of the table, and that precious status symbol, the salt-cellar, was placed midway down the table to form a boundary of distinction between the distinguished guests and those of more humble rank. Those on the wrong side of the salt often had to be content with tables at floor level, and it is from this custom that we get the dictum 'he sits below the salt', denoting a man of little social importance.

It was important not to trespass beyond this boundary as a satirist wrote:

> *Thou are a carle of mean degree,*
> *Ye salte yt stands twain me and thee.*

An attempt to slip across the boundary could be met by a pelting with half-picked bones thrown by the exalted whose birth was doubtless better than their table manners. However, it could happen that a guest from the wrong side of the barrier would be asked to sit on the right side, this being a recognized sign of improved social status. Equally, a more noble guest might be placed on the lower end of the table, sent there in disgrace for committing a misdemeanour.

Another advantage of being on the right side of the salt was that the wine was circulated frequently only above the salt; and the dishes served below the salt were of a coarser quality than those served above.

Salt was taken with a knife by the gentlefolk, and with the fingers by the common people. Salt spoons had not been invented.

Each person had his own smaller salt in front of him. The very poor had no salt-cellars at all: they used a bit of the trencher bread, scooping out a hole in the middle and putting their salt into this.

There are some of the old salt-cellars still in existence. In the Tower of London, among the Crown Jewels, there is a salt-cellar known as Queen Elizabeth's Great Salt-Cellar, a splendid object twelve inches high with a pan on top to hold the salt, over which is a golden canopy to prevent dust from polluting the salt. A famous existing Charles I salt-cellar, two feet high, is in the shape of a turreted castle. There are the so-called St George's salts in varying shapes, each one surmounted by a figure of the saintly knight in armour. Finally, there is a salt in the form of a huntsman bearing on his head a container made of rock crystal for holding salt, which belongs to All Soul's College, Oxford.

Gradually salt-cellars changed from the massive interesting and social pieces they were to those made during the reigns of Queen Anne and George I, which were plain but had charm of style. By 1740 the now familiar bowl on its three or four legs became the pattern and has remained popular until today. In between there were flights of fancy among the designers of salt-cellars. There were the fanciful Adam-designed salt-cellars of the late eighteenth century; some French rococo salt-cellars of a later date; a boat-shaped salt-cellar was popular in the later eighteenth century, and what one might call novelty designs became fashionable at the beginning of the Regency.

An English dinner under the Protectorate. The large salt-cellar was carefully positioned.

Trenchers and Roundels

Trenchers were the forerunners of our plates and were used in England from medieval days until as late as the period of Charles II for banquets. The first trenchers were slabs of coarse bread made from unsifted flour. The bread was four days old before cut into shape, usually square, with a trencher knife. The crusts were pared off and thrown to the dogs. The food, usually meat, was placed on the trencher as we place our meat upon a plate. Sometimes when the meal was finished the trencher would be eaten, but usually when it became soggy it would be removed and replaced. The number of times the trencher was changed during a meal depended on a person's rank or status. The soggy trencher was either given to the prowling dogs or dropped into a voider or voyder (a large dish used to remove scraps) and given as alms to the poor. Since diners also wiped their greasy fingers on their trenchers, one does not dwell on the thoughts of the deserving poor receiving these doubtful offerings. (Incidentally, off the kitchen of some large houses there was an almsroom.)

The name trencher was then given to square wooden plates with a rim for salt. These remained in use from the sixteenth century to the early nineteenth in every cottage and farmhouse. Examples of these can be seen in folk museums, also in Anne Hathaway's cottage at Stratford-on-Avon. Later trenchers were rounded.

Wooden trenchers were also known as treen roundels and were usually made from beech, sycamore or white maple wood. These came into use after the fifteenth century. The word treen is interesting and worth a small *divertissement*. Derived from the Middle English *tre* or *tree*, treen was used to describe a large number of small wooden items used daily in kitchens and dining rooms. Generally, a form of peasant art, treen work was well turned and carved. Although intended for practical use, some treen pieces were elaborately decorated and as they were individually carved, it was seldom that two pieces were alike. Today they are valued by passionate collectors of household equipment, flattering to those men of long ago who turned and carved them so lovingly.

From bread to wood, then to pewter, to tin (made to look like silver), and finally to silver: these were the easy steps. By the late Georgian period the average well-to-do home in England had its silver plates and dishes, often reserved for special occasions. But both pewter and wooden trenchers were still in use, especially in the homes of the poorer people.

The early wooden trenchers were about 9 inches in diameter, and those were turned on a lathe. Their shape and size were copied by the silversmiths and later the potters, so that today, although we eat off a plate we can in effect say we eat off trenchers. (The word was taken from the Old French *trancher*, to cut.) Some people still talk of a bread trencher, meaning the piece of wood on which we rest our bread. There was also a butter trencher, a small piece of wood placed in the bottom of a butter dish.

By 1580 elaborate and fancy trenchers were in vogue. Some were gilded, some had little verses, epigrams and proverbs spelt out on their reverse sides, with such topics as Biblical texts, Aesop's fables, the language of flowers etc. Such trenchers were also used for biscuits and sugar conceits (facetious subjects, signs of the zodiac etc. moulded in sugar), or marchpanes (a kind of marzipan biscuit) or caraway biscuits, which were served with wine.

The Victoria and Albert Museum has several sets of these trenchers or roundels. One set consists of botanical illustrations printed on paper and pasted on. These were used at New Year parties and it was intended that each guest should turn over his roundel and read out the inscription. Some of the sets made around 1610 were done in black Indian-style design inspired by the East India Company. They continued to be fashionable until about 1630. The present-day heat-proof table mats are not dissimilar.

Some of the customs of our ancestors made for economy in the serving of food, for two people often shared the same trencher. They might be two friends, as an act of chivalrous courtesy, sometimes even a knight and his

Illustration from early Tudor times showing the simplicity of a meal at a humble inn.

lady, or a man and wife. It was a tradition continued as late as 1752 by the Duke and Duchess of Hamilton who ate off the same plate at the end of their table.

It is also interesting to observe that maple wood trenchers were still seen in the days of Queen Victoria and used by the seventy scholars at Winchester. These were usually hollow on both sides so that meat was eaten off one side, then it was wiped clean (we hope) and turned over for the pudding to be served. These boards are somewhat similar in design to our present-day bread boards.

Towards the end of the seventeenth century wooden trenchers and bowls gave way to earthenware, and china plates were seen everywhere. But it has been observed that the trencher did not die willingly, and now they are respected museum pieces.

The Kitchen and its Equipment

It is interesting that in earlier times kitchen equipment was regarded as valuable property, and great care was taken of the many pots and pans of noblemen. They were carried in carts as part of their 'running' wardrobe when they travelled to their various manors; it is recorded that Edward I carried his kitchen equipment with him whenever he went from Langley to his manor in Isenhamsted.

Some of the kitchen utensils of Edward III were rated with the royal jewels. Such articles were indeed often made from silver, for example, silver pans were used for the frying of lampreys and other dainty dishes. But, curiously, most of the utensils recorded among Edward III's effects were mentioned as made of iron.

An inventory of King Henry V's kitchen equipment lists spits or 'broches' made of silver, probably because it was the custom to take them to the table complete with the joint or fowl which had been roasted on the spit. We get some idea of the value accorded to these pots and pans when we read ancient wills in which solemn mention is made of the pots and pans bequeathed to sons and daughters.

During the Middle Ages, the kitchen was a temporary affair connected by a passage leading to the minor offices. Later, with a generally more settled way of life, the kitchen became more important, indeed, so important that it was built next to the great hall, complete with pantry and buttery. Some of the larger kitchens in castles and manor houses were splendid, with capacious hearths and a brilliant array of shining pots and pans. A well-equipped kitchen would boast several tables, one for coping with the large joints of meat, a smaller one for shredding cabbages and other vegetables. There would be a cheese container and another for bread called an 'ark' or chest. In 1341 the will of one Thomas Harpham records that his daughter was left an 'ark' which had belonged to her mother. The same term was found again in 1559, and in the north of England the word in 1861 still meant a large chest. There was also a large sieve for sieving or 'boulting' the flour; and a coffer filled with spices. Cutlery was kept in the pantry.

Most kitchens had a lot of wooden utensils. There were mortars and pestles, frying pans of several shapes called skillets and posnets; there were

A variety of metal cooking vessels, each made for a specific purpose.

baskets, spits of various sizes, pickling vats, platters, trenchers, roundels etc., pewter measures and usually what would be regarded today as an interesting collection of gingerbread and marchpane moulds as well as waffle pans or irons.

Attached to the kitchen was the saltery where the meats were cured, the ewery in which lavers and towels were stored, the saucery for the platters and cups, and the squillery or scullery where dishes were washed and the trenchers scraped by the trencher knaves. Ovens were only found in really large houses. Bellows, thought to have been introduced by the Germans in the sixteenth century, were important and were decorated with mottoes such as, 'As the sparks do upward fly, Think that thou has trouble nigh.' However, whatever connection the Germans may have had with the introduction of the bellows, it was recorded in 1463 that John Baret left his niece Janet 'a peyr of belwys'.

An amusing and popular item in many kitchens was a red jug with many spouts sticking out at all angles, called a Wiltshire puzzle jug. The object of the spouts was for the drinker to extract the contents of the jug without spilling any, and to do this he had to know which of the many spouts his fingers had to cover, also to find the concealed hole in the handle of the jug.

APPLE CORERS AND CHEESE SCOOPS Many of these have been found on Roman remains. They were made from sheep's shanks, carefully carved and pared to the shape of scoops. They were especially common in Oxfordshire and the Yorkshire Dales.

CAT A form of trivet which was made up of six spokes springing from a central body, three at the top and three at the bottom. It could be used either side up and was called a cat because however it fell, it always landed like a cat on its feet.

CAULDRON or COOKING POT This was one of the oldest forms of kitchen utensil. Most of the earliest cauldrons were made of iron but some were made of bronze. Usually they had three feet, a half-loop handle and often a lip from which the liquid in the pot was poured. They were used for all kinds of cooking and varied in size from very large to small. As most early illustrations show, they were suspended from a hanger or a tripod over an open fire.

Meat was often boiled in such pots instead of being roasted, and a common method in cottages was to cook various foods in the pot at the same time. The cottagers would immerse small earthenware pots, filled with food and sealed with watertight covers, in the pot, and hang their beans and other vegetables held in net bags round the inside of the cauldron. Or the pots could be used as an oven for baking cakes or bread. It could be inverted and ashes heaped round it. Bread baked in this manner was called 'upset bread'. The pots were also stood on the hearth, tightly lidded or covered with an iron plate, ashes heaped on the top to bake the 'pot oven bread'.

CHIMNEY CRANE Cooking pots were suspended from a ratchet hanger. This had an adjustable hook either hung from an iron bar, placed horizontally across the chimney, or suspended from a crane fixed to the side of the fire. The earliest cranes were made of wood and later of iron, often by the blacksmith. Some are fine examples of craftsmanship. When fixed into position these cranes could swivel to and fro in a horizontal plane to any desired position. Most were utilitarian but some were elaborately decorated.

COUVRE FEU For centuries it was the custom never to let the fire completely die out, and a cover or *couvre feu* was used to cover the glowing embers at night so that they remained alight until morning. It also prevented the house from catching fire. A good blow with the bellows first thing in the morning had the fire quickly restored.

FORKS These were used for cooking but not for eating. There was a so-called toasting fork, a two-pronged rack socketed to the end of a wooden handle.

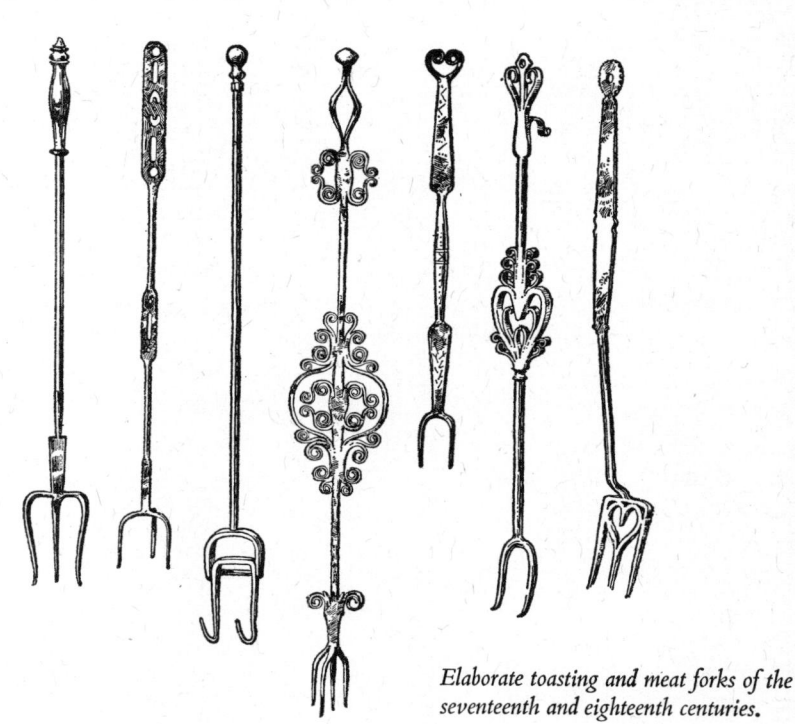

Elaborate toasting and meat forks of the seventeenth and eighteenth centuries.

FRYING PAN Most of these had wrought iron handles at least three feet long to enable the cook to stand well away from the fire when working.

GRATE The use of grates indoors is comparatively recent, since early grates or fires were made for outdoor use. Large roasting grates began in Queen Elizabeth I's time and these had moveable sides so that the fire could be adjusted to the size of the joint. In cottage kitchens there was a kind of portable fire called a 'duck's egg' which was used in the early eighteenth and nineteenth centuries. It had no oven and was a low cast-iron grate standing twelve inches from the ground and could be fired with either wood or coal.

GRIDIRON or GRIDDLE One of the oldest of our cooking utensils, this has been in common use since medieval days for cooking on or near an open fire. The early gridirons had extra long handles so that they could rest on a baking iron or over the top grate of a fire. They were of various shapes, round, square or even diamond. One version was developed with grooved bars to let the hot fat and gravy trickle into a transverse trough next to the handle.

KETTLE TILTER This was a type of hanger with two hooks to hold the handle of a kettle. It was so constructed that water could be poured from the kettle without lifting it up or dirtying the hands. It was also called a 'lazy-back' or an 'idle-back'.

LARD BEATING TABLE Lard-making was one of the processes carried out in a farmhouse kitchen. The leaf or flay from the pig was placed on the table and beaten with a lard beater, a heavy steel poker, until the lard was soft. It took two men a whole day to beat the lard.

MEAT HOOKS These were adjustable hooks from which meat was suspended and held in front of the fire for roasting. Most of them were simple, but later a caliper type of hook was invented which proved to be somewhat complicated.

MORTARS AND PESTLES Stoneware mortars have been found among Roman remains, but not pestles, which would suggest the latter were made of wood. Mortars were used in much the same way in which we use our mixing bowls, but also with the pestle for powdering spices or nuts. They varied considerably in size, and an average kitchen would have more than one. There was a type with its own stand, and an over-sized example of this can be seen in the Pavilion kitchen at Brighton.

OVEN Brick ovens for baking bread were a common feature in old farmhouses and better-class cottages. They were built into the side of the hearth in the walls of the fireplace and were arched like a tunnel, projecting from the farm or cottage like a domed semicircle. The mouth of the oven had a 'stopper' or door which in early days was made of solid oak, later of iron. It fitted tightly and had two handles so that it could be removed from the oven. The oven was heated with faggots of brushwood and logs which were placed on the floor of the oven before baking began. When the oven was hot enough, the wood was scraped out with a scraper, shaped like a hoe. (Similar ovens can still be seen in Italy used for making *pizze*.) Baking was done once a week in the stored-up heat of the oven. Small cakes and biscuits were baked first, followed by pies and foods cooked in batter. Finally came the bread. Some loaves were cooked in tins, others such as cottage loaves, were simply placed on the floor of the oven. The dough was put into the oven by means of an oven peel (q.v.) for the ovens sent out a tremendous heat.

The ovens took a good two hours to heat, and baking went on all day. When it was finished, herbs and fruits were put into the oven to dry, also fresh wood to dry against the next baking day. Those who were too poor to own such an oven did their baking on bakestones or gridirons.

OVEN FORK This was used for stacking the baking ovens and the major part of the fork was made of metal which resisted the heat better than wood. They were several feet long.

OVEN PEEL A shovel or spade-shaped utensil with an immensely long handle (often six or seven feet long) used by bakers from medieval times until the eighteenth and even nineteenth centuries – and still by Italian bakers in their *pizze* ovens. In Warwickshire peels were shorter because of the shallow local ovens.

PIPKIN See SKILLET.

PLATE WARMERS These were made of pewter and stood in front of the fire on iron stands. Later a type of Dutch oven was used for plate warming.

POSNET See SKILLET.

POT HOOKS or HANGERS These were a necessity in every kitchen. Usually they were made of iron and of one piece and were used for hanging pots from the chimney cranes or bars. Some elaborate forms in three or four pieces were in use in medieval times which had a rack and loop so that the height of the pot above the fire could be adjusted as required. In some of the later types there was provision for a rotary movement. They were also called cotrails, jibcrooks and trammelles.

RATCHET HANGER This was an iron bar curved at the top with a flat iron sheet ratchet attachment similar to a coarse saw. The hooked end of the upright passed over a wooden chimney bar, the lower end had a hook suspended from a loop which could be caught in the teeth of the rachet.

SALAMANDER This consisted of a long wrought iron handle at the end of which was a square or round plate, about an inch thick, used for browning the top of various foods. The plate was placed in the fire until it became red-hot and then held close to the food which quickly browned. Older salamanders have short legs fixed to the stem to support the plate for use on a low hearth.

SKILLET This was used in the earliest forms of cooking and in medieval times for cooking over an open fire. It looked like a bronze cauldron with a handle attached to the rim and three legs to the base so that it could stand in the hearth in the embers. By the sixteenth and seventeenth centuries its shape had altered so much that the opening was larger than the base, and it looked more like our modern saucepan.

Skillets were made of bell metal and more than likely by bell makers. The average skillet was some 7 in. in diameter with a $9\frac{1}{2}$ in. long handle. It held three pints and weighed 7 lb. Skillets were also called pipkins and posnets.

SPITS A small book could be written on the history and evolution of the roasting spit. As the earliest form of cooking was roasting in front of an open fire, most of the meat was roasted on a spit or broche as it was also called. The spit was of hard wood, often hazel, sharpened at both ends and laid upon two wooden crutches, placed in front of the fire. The first spits were simple rods, but in time a handle was attached to it to make the turning easier. Later on, spits were made of wrought iron with one end of the spit in the form of a handle. This was turned by a boy known as a turnspit. Later models introduced a wheel at one end.

In the seventeenth century dogs were made to turn the spit. The unhappy dogs were no doubt diligent, for we are told that a piece of hot coal was laid at their heels to keep them running. As a joint of meat could take up to three hours in roasting, it is no wonder that the dogs had 'a suspicious look about them, as if they were weary of the task they had to do'. However, other authorities report that the dogs liked the warmth, and the titbits which they were thrown. Ugly, long-bodied, bandy-legged dogs, they are said to be the forerunners of the present Basset hounds.

Other methods were invented to turn spits, some of a Heath Robinson complexity. There was the 'spit-jack', a weight-driven spit, considered in the sixteenth century as a labour-saving device. There was the 'smoke-jack', worked by means of a fan in the chimney; also the 'basket-spit' in which a whole joint of an animal could be placed which sometimes had a small iron hook on which small items could be secured. After the smoke-jack, there were the dangle-spit, the bottle-jack and the spring-driven spit, all coming in after the seventeenth century.

TOASTERS There were two main types of toaster used on every hearth. One was for bread, the other for meat. They both stood on three short legs but the bread toaster had a contrivance similar to a toast rack, which revolved so that both sides of the bread could be toasted. The meat toaster had a tray underneath it to collect the drippings and was also provided with a fork to turn or remove the meat with ease.

TRIVET An iron stand which supported cooking pots when they were taken off the fire. Some trivets consisted of three legs attached to a round iron plate, and these were intended only for standing in the hearth. Others were made to hang from the fire bars, but these often too had iron bars so they could perform a dual service. Some trivets could also be pushed into the fire and used for cooking.

A mechanical 'three-footed' spit, geared to turn the meat at different speeds at each level.

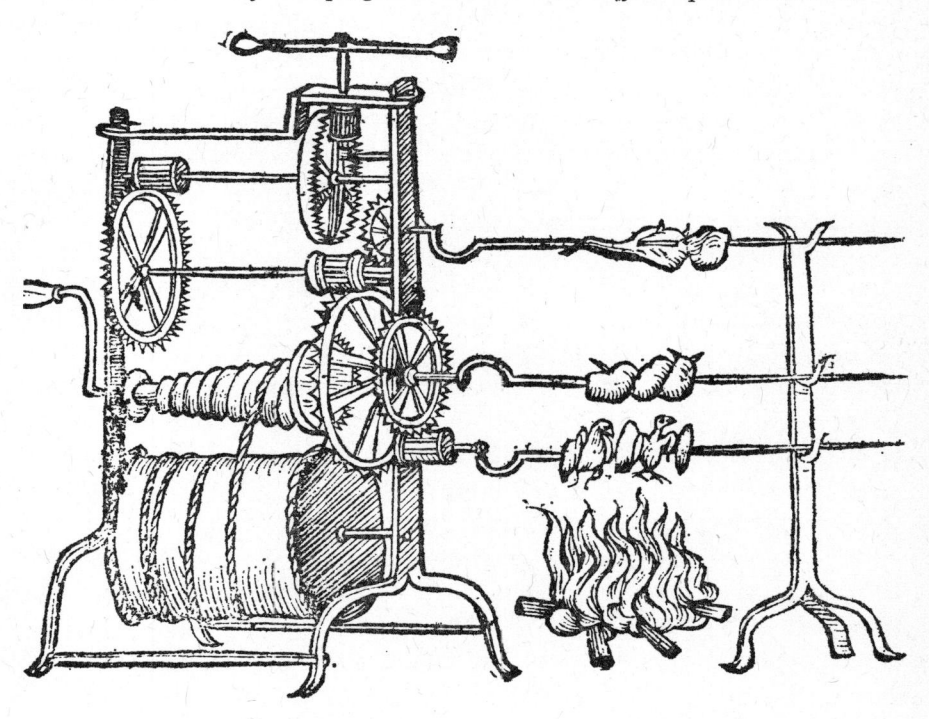

Old Cookery Books

The first printed English cookery book came off the Caxton press in 1500. Between that time and 1600 another seventeen books on cooking were published.

Many of these old works contained a wealth of knowledge which throws light on the culinary habits of our ancestors, their deep-bred superstitions, their food fears and their ignorance. Instructions were offered for running the household competently, hints on gardening, marketing, etiquette, the setting of the table, etc. Sometimes it seemed as if the giving of recipes was but incidental.

The earliest written work on cookery in Britain was by Alexander Neckham. He was born in 1157 and was a 'milk brother' of Prince Richard. A distinguished teacher with a passion for writing long lists of words, his book enumerates many kinds of food available at that time, as well as essentials for the kitchen. *Treatise de Utensibilis*, the book, of which several manuscript copies still exist, was designed as a kind of popular textbook aimed as much to teach his students to read as to manage the house or to cook; it was written in a kind of French with a few English words intermixed.

This was followed by probably the best known of the old cookery books, *The Forme of Cury* (see page 70), compiled by the master cooks of Richard II whom they hailed as the 'best and ryallest' eater of all Christian kings. And well they might, for the king was famous for his prodigious entertaining. He appears to have been the first of our kings to have gained any sort of reputation as a gourmet, and is said to have had 2,000 cooks.

Another famous old manuscript is the *Liber Cure Cocorum* (see pages 71–72), and this, unlike most of the books, does offer some recipes at the end, for the poor. These are mainly instructions for cooking vegetables of which neither the rich nor the poor had much opinion.

Many of these early manuscripts show a remarkable similarity – there was no such thing as a copyright law, and often were lavishly and amusingly illustrated. Many show drawings of the cooks at work. Some are shown sitting down to their work in front of the fire, 'cooking leisurely'. As much of the early cooking took a long time on those open fires, it was important to be comfortable as one watched the pot a-boiling. One illustration shows a cook comfortably seated reading a book (of recipes?): Another is shown stirring her pot while a wily priest kisses her and, behind her back, steals from the pot.

The titles of the early cookery books are delightful, at times simple and at times positively conceited. There is the emphatically titled *This is the Boke of Cokery*, printed in 1500. A little later in 1508 *Here Begyneth the Boke of Kervynge* by Wynkyn de Worde was printed (de Worde wrote a carol for the Boar's Head Feast at Oxford University). *The Castel of Helth* appeared in 1539, and in 1596 came *The Good Huswifes Jewell*, which offers 'most excellent and rare Deuises for conceites in Cookery, found out by the practise of Thomas Dawson'. Book after book followed, all with similar titles, 'Delightes', 'Rare Closets', 'Rich Cabinets', 'Compleat Cooks' etc.

Between 1609 – when *Delightes for Ladies* by Sir Hugh Plat was published (reprinted in 1948) – and 1700, some 45 more cookery books were published and, an interesting fact, more cookery books were produced in England at that time than anywhere else.

In 1620 Tobias Venner (*see* page 83) published his so-called 'cottage cookery book' *Via Recta ad Vitam Longam*, which is as much concerned with dietary precepts as with cooking. He was a practising physician and by no means the only one to write a cookery book. We have the 'masterpiece' of Sir Kenelm Digby or Sir Kenelme Digbie (*see* page 84), and much later, in the early nineteenth century, Dr Kitchiner, physician and man-about-town who wrote *The Best Books of Cookery* as well as *The Cook's Oracle*.

In 1656 appeared another of these cookery-medical books, published in three parts. Part One was *The Queen's Closet Opened or the Pearl of Practise*, which gave medical advice and receipts. Part Two ran: *A Queen's Delight, or The Art of Preserving, Conserving, and Candying, as also a Right Knowledge of Making Perfumes and Distilling the Most Excellent Waters*. Part Three was called: *The Compleat Cook, Expertly Prescribing the most ready ways, whether Italian, Spanish or French, for Dressing of Flesh and Fish, Ordering of Sauces or Making of Pastry*: the sort of cookery book in fact which at that time was probably declared a cookery book to end all cookery books.

In the same year came *The Perfect Marnette (French Cook)* and more of those books for 'Ladies and Gentlewomen' all intent on making Lumber Pye and Other Tarts, and roasting larks or preparing sauces for 'fieldfare, rabbets and Capon'.

The year 1664 witnessed the publication of *The Court & Kitchin of Elizabeth called Joan Cromwell, the Wife of the late Usurper, truly Described and Represented, and now Made Publick for general Satisfaction*. The frontispiece is a picture of the lady looking sadly severe, yet curiously a grinning monkey peers over her shoulder. Beneath the picture is a cautionary poem:

From feigned glory & Usurped Throne
And all the greatnesse to me falsly shown
And from the Arts of Government set free
See how Protectresse and a Drudge agree.

Elizabeth (Joan) Cromwell may well have known how to write on cookery and sensible housekeeping, but it is doubtful that she wrote this little book. More probably it was a scurrilous Royalist attempt to poke fun at the Cromwells, who were reputed to have been parsimonious in the extreme. But the book curiously does give some excellent recipes for dishes which apparently made their appearance on the Cromwell table, such as Dutch Pudding and Scotch Collops.

Possibly the most oft repeated story of Cromwell and his wife is the one which shows that he, who might be master of his Parliament, was not of his table. Asking one day for an orange to eat with his roast veal, he was tartly informed that 'an orange cost a groat and for her part she never intended to give it'.

Whether parsimonious or not, the little book does point out that the couple gave much to the poor. It seems that eight stone of beef was cooked every morning and all the scraps collected and given to the hungry poor, who had no State relief.

A spate of cookery books, all emphasizing rather splendid cooking followed, *Court Cookery, Court and Country Cooking*, and so on, nearly all written by men. Hannah Woolley seems to have been the one lone female writer in this field. Her book was somewhat grandly called *The Queen-like Closet: or Rich Cabinet Stored with all manner of rare Receipts for Preserving, Candying, and Cookery. Very pleasant and beneficial to all ingenious persons of the female sex*. Hannah Woolley (sometimes spelt Woley) was a letter writer and an industrious woman. The book, first published in 1670, was well put together and contains menus, directions to servants, as well as recipes. A fifth edition was published in 1684.

As the years passed titles became meaner, or probably the cost of living was rising and royal cooking was becoming too expensive. The year 1795 produced such titles as *The Frugal Housewife, The Economical Housewife* etc.

Old cookery books are becoming increasingly rare and a great many are now being purchased by American collectors. There are several private collections of old cookery books; one of the most important in Britain belonged to the late André L. Simon and includes some very rare volumes indeed.

THE FORME OF CURY
A ROLL OF ANCIENT ENGLISH COOKERY

*Compiled circa AD 1390
by the Master-Cooks of King Richard II*

This manuscript is one of the earliest recorded works on English cookery and probably one of the best known. It is a singular relic of the times, for it is yards of vellum rolled up to the thickness of the average rolling pin. It has seven joins of membrane with blue zigzag stitching. The printing is in black and red. The first yard is so faded as to be indecipherable, but further down one can read the old script perfectly clearly.

W. Carew Hazlitt, in *Old Cookery Books* (1886) wrote: '*The Forme of Cury* will amply remunerate a study. It presents the earliest mention so far as I can discern of olive oil, cloves, mace and gourds.'

The roll contains recipes dating from the time of William the Conqueror to that of Richard II, a period of some three hundred years. Many of the dishes have names of Anglo-Saxon derivation but the nomenclature is in Norman French.

Still quoting Hazlitt, *The Forme of Cury* is the *codex princips* in the long and extensive catalogue of works on English cookery, and contains 196 receipts, commencing with a Table of Contents and a kind of preamble. It is interesting to include its little introduction as it does illustrate the custom in those days of consulting medical opinion in matters culinary – an ancient alliance. It runs:

> ... forme of cury (cookery) was compiled of the chef maistes cokes of Kyng Richard the Secund aftir the conquest, the which was accounted the best and ryallest vyand (nice eater) af alle cften yn ynges (Christian kings); and it was compiled by assent and avysement of maisters and phisik and of philosophie that dwellid in his court. First it techith a man for to make commune pottages and commune meetis for howshold, as they should be made craftly and holsomly. Aftirward it techith for to make curious potages of states, both hye and lowe. And the techying of the forme of making potages and of meetes, both of flesh and of fissh, buth (are) y settle here by noumbre and by order.

The Roll purports to enable a man 'to make commpottages and common meats for the household, as they should be made, craftly and wholesomely', in other words, the book was not intended entirely for royalty.

There is a Saracen sauce (*see* page 92), possibly a recipe that came to

England with the returning Crusaders, pig with sage stuffing, messes of almonds, peas and beans. White grease is called for in some of the recipes but not butter. The mention of sugar suggests that it was becoming more generally used. Herbs and spices were naturally in great demand, sometimes to add flavour, but almost as often to mask odour. Fruits, like quince, which had its own distinct flavour, were cooked with honey and a variety of spices, such as ginger, almonds, saffron and even egg yolks. One wonders how the quince flavour survived all this.

The manuscript copy of *The Forme of Cury* is now in the British Museum. It had been presented to Queen Elizabeth I in 1586 by Lord Stafford. Later it became the property of the Earl of Oxford and was acquired at a sale of his manuscripts by James West. It then went to Gustavius Brander, Curator of the British Museum. In 1780 it attracted the attention of Samuel Pegge, the well-known antiquarian, who wrote about the manuscript and published in 1780 a full transcript of the roll with some valuable comments, an index and a glossary.

LIBER CURE COCORUM

Fifteenth Century

This book which contains 127 recipes in verse is to be found in the British Museum. It is considered to have been written about the time of Henry VI, probably in a northern dialect. It presents for the most part much that had been written already in earlier treatises in more comprehensive forms. Even so, this little book is important for it adds to our knowledge of how the tables of middle-class Englishmen were furnished, rather than the royal tables or those of the nobility.

The poetical ability of the author leaves much to be desired at times, and W. C. Hazlitt notes that in the receipt 'for a service on a fish-day' the reader is prayed within four lines, to cover his white herring for God's sake, and lay his mustard over his red for God's love, all because sake and love rhyme with take and above.

The following verses from *Liber Cure Cocorum* have been partially translated.

FOR CAPONS IN ERBIS

First stuff your capons with saveray,
With parsley, a little, hissop I say;
Then take the neck, remove the bone;
And make a pudding thereof at once
With an egg and minced bread also
With hacked liver and heart there to
With powder of pepper and saffron; then
Sew fast the bill [sic] great end, I ken (command)
Then boil the capon, as I they say,
With parsley, sage, hissop, saveray,
A little nep, bruise it in haste (catmint)
And breake it in two; in it you cast
With slices of bacon, enbrawded here (garnished or embroidered)
And colour your broth with saffron dear
When it is boiled, in dish it lay
The bacon, the neck beside it in fay (faith)
Take ground saffron tempered with ale
To flourish your capon with cider you shall
Lying in dish, and serve it then,
Set it in hall before good men.

FOR A CAWDELL

Break ten eggs in a cup full fair
Do away the white without diswayre (doubt)
Your string also thou put away
And swing thy yolks with spoon, I thee say;
Then mix them wel with good ale,
A cupfull large take thou shall
Set it on (the) fire, stir it, I tell,
Beware therewith that it never welle (boils)
If thou cast salt thereto, iwys (certainly)
Thou mars all, so have I blis. (I tell you truly)

[72]

THE GOVERNAYLE OF HEALTHE:
WITH THE MEDECYNE OF THE STOMACKE
circa 1490

The author of this book, the first printed book on diet, is unknown. It is the least known and most rare of all Caxton's productions. Consisting of seventeen pages, most of the work is written in stanzas, a usual practice of the time, in order to assist the reader in the memorizing of the advice.

Much of the content is a free translation of the work *Regimen Sanitatis Salernitanum*. Over the centuries the *Regimen* had been frequently plagiarized. In this Caxton edition doctors are described as leches, but it is more probable that this expression refers to the word lesche or leech for slicing and carving. Medicine is described as leachecraft, and therefore a surgeon would be a leche.

Naturally Galen (AD 130–201) is much quoted in the booklet and, roughly translated, his advice on how to live healthfully indicates seven things are necessary:

1 *Discreet choice of food and drink*
2 *Wilful bodily exercise before food until one becomes hot and short of breath*
3 *Everything eaten to be chewed up small*
4 *To eat only when one has an appetite*
5 *To sleep on in the morning until one awakes naturally*
6 *To take no meat while emotionally upset; but when happy as much as desired*
7 *To use saffron with food, as it aids digestion, keeps one young, happy and fit.*

These small pearls of advice, some of which are still valid today, were followed by recommendations that after exercise one should take a little fresh wheat bread, well baked and rather sour, then a draught of good clear wine. One should not eat unless feeling hungry, except perhaps to take a little good warm meat to provoke the appetite.

However, it was not considered wise to eat until one felt sure that a previous meal had been digested, and never to eat things which are disliked – a piece of advice millions of children would cherish.

Foods are described as hot and cold. Hot foods are pepper, garlic, onion, cress, sage, mint and parsley. These warm the blood. Cold foods freshen the blood and consist of lettuce, purslane, gourdes etc.

Watery foods such as melon and cucumber meet with disapproval; but recommended are year-old lambs, kids, sucking calves, hens, capons, chickens, partridges, plovers, pheasants, small birds of the field and wood, but *not* of the water; also young rabbits and pigs' feet, and scaled fish of running water, and raw eggs. Other recommendations are: salt and sour meats can be 'amended' with sweet apples, and sweet meats with honey and good old wine. Fruit, such as cherries, grapes and almonds, should be eaten before meat; after meat, pears, quinces and nuts, especially walnuts are suggested.

Galenic teaching was that fruits could give rise to fevers, and the writer claimed his own father lived a hundred years because he never ate fruit. The author of the *Governayle*, while not quite so rigid on the matter of fruits, did advise: 'an' fro fruits, hold thyn abstynence', adding that peaches (if you must eat fruit) do the least harm and, in any case, those who ate sparingly lived longer than the gluttons. Galen is again quoted as saying that people should not eat diverse foods; and if they do, the next morning they should fast solely on bread, and in the evening on meat alone.

Aucien is quoted as recommending eleven hours' break between meals, and only eating three times in two days, e.g. twice today and once tomorrow, and always to take a walk after meals.

The author himself recommends *pesen pottage* (pease soup) as a useful medicine and gives instructions for its preparation. His treatment for overeating is to have a mouth wash of oil and water combined, then to fast and sleep for twenty-four hours, then take but a little food with wine, and on the third day exercise and bathe:

> *For helth of body covers for* (from) *colde they hede,*
> *Ete no rawe mete, take good hede thereto*
> *Drynke holsom wyne fede the on lyght brede,*
> *Wyth an appetyte ryse from they mete also . . .*
>
> *Moderate food gyveth to man his healthe,*
> *And all surfetes doth from hym remeve.*

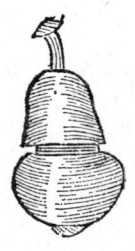

Directions to the cook for carving pears in intricate designs.

THE BOKE OF KERVYNGE

by Wynkyn de Worde

1508

This was the first book printed in England concerned entirely with 'the table'. A short book of only twenty-four pages, it is nevertheless a beautiful little volume. Several later editions appeared until the year 1613. Probably its chief claim to fame is its page on carving. This has been quoted in nearly all historical books on cookery, ever since the work was first published.

The carver in de Worde's day was an important and indispensable official. Large quantities of meat, poultry and game were consumed at banquets and all was carved by the carver. Wynkyn de Worde therefore sets out his duties minutely in his book or, as one writer said, with an 'almost ecclesiastical solemnity befitting his great task'.

The carver, who was a man of high dignity, had his important instructions, and nothing was left to chance. He was expected to know all the technical terms as elucidated by de Worde and also to know 'the fair handling of a knife' on which he should put only two fingers and a thumb. In his left hand he had a trencher to hold the meat, since there were no forks. Upon 'fish, flesh, beast or fowl' he should use no more than two fingers and a thumb to keep them in position and naturally never smear the tablecloth with his knife but wipe it with his napkin especially provided.

The following examples of carving are typical of his instructions:

DYSPLAYE THAT CRANE Take a crane and unfolde his leggs, and cut of his wynges by the joyntes; then take up his wynges and his legges and sauce hym with poudres of gynger, mustard, vynegre, and salte.

TAYME THAT CRABBE A crabbe, break him asunder in a dish, make the shel clean and put in the stuf again, temper it with vynegre and poudres, then cover it with bread and send it to the kitchen to heat, then set it to your sovereign and break the great claws and lay them in a dish.

We have hardly changed this method even today.

Having dealt precisely with the carver, the author then instructs the butler and the panter in their duties, again in detail. The carver, it is also explained, must have spent at least one year in these capacities. The panter was the 'keeper and cutter-up of bread', for which he must possess three sharp knives: one to square the trencher loaves, another to be used as a 'clipper', and the third to make the trenchers smooth. Trencher bread was required to be four days old so that it cut with a good sharp edge. The master's bread was 'chipped' while still hot, while the household bread was three days old. Bread served at table had to be cut, not broken, and the crusts removed. Why this was so no one knows. Maybe the bread was burnt and the crusts too hard for the teeth of that period.

The knives must be polished and the spoons kept clean. The cloths, towels and napkins kept folded in a closet or on a 'perch'. The salt should be planed with an ivory plane 2 in. broad and 3 in. long. The salt-cellar lid should never touch the salt.

At all seasons butter, cheese, apples, pears, nuts, plums, grapes, dates, figs, raisins, compost (a sort of mincemeat pickle), green ginger and chardequince (quince jam) were to be kept in the larder. And for feasting, there must be butter, plums, damsons, cherries and grapes. After a meal, pears, nuts, strawberries (these were wild and not garden strawberries), whortleberries and hard cheese, also apples and caraway comfits were served.

It was also the job of the butler and panter to look after the wine cellar, and this too is described in detail. A number of the wines then in use are named: red wine, white wine, and claret wine; osey or osaye, capryke, capolet, Rhine wine, Malmesey, Bastard or Bastarde, Tyre, Romney or Romanyke, Muscadell, Clare, Raspys, Vernage wyne cut. There is also a lengthy description on how to make Hippocras which was to be served with wafers.

Table-laying came next and is dealt with in the same detail. It is carefully explained how to arrange several pieces of cloth in different directions, the coloured edges of which, it is stressed, should appear at the front of the table. The tablecloths were also meant to protect the legs of the diners from draughts.

Instructions for carving a suckling pig.

When laying the table, the butler is instructed to put a towel round his neck and another on his arm. On his left arm he was expected to carry seven loaves of bread and four trencher loaves, as well as the salts. In his right hand he held the napkins, also the knives and spoons. The salt was laid on the right side of the master, and the trenchers on the left, with spoons and folded napkins. The master was served with four or five trenchers in the course of a meal; those of lower degree, fewer. The butler also found in this exact little book instructions on how to clear the table. He had to arrange on a sort of sideboard, or at every place on the table, ewers of hot and cold water, and bowls for diners to wash their hands, both before and after the meal.

After the butler's duties came the instructions for the sewer or server and the carver, two different officials.

The server had to discuss with the cook daily what was to be served so that he had the table properly organized, with enough waiters to carry the dishes. For the service of the meat, he is told to take the knife in his hand and cut the meat in the dish and lay it on the master's trencher. He sees there is mustard.

Frumenty (one of the oldest dishes dating from Saxon times) was cut into seven slices with a knife. Peas and bacon, beef chine and mutton were served minced into the sauce. Meat must be carved into four slices for each morsel so that the master can dip them into the sauce. There are also instructions on the serving of whole fowl and beasts. Hot pies are to be opened at the top, cold ones in the middle, and custards 'checked' into squares.

And the following list of how to deal with the various foods surely adds regret that such expressions are no longer in daily use.

Breke that dere	*chyne that samon*	*alaye that fesande*
lesche y brawne	*strynge that lampraye*	*wynge that partryche*
rere that goose	*splatte that pyke*	*wynge that quayle*
lyst that swanne	*sauce that playce*	*mynce that plover*
sauce that capon	*sauce that tenche*	*thye that pegyon*
spoyle that henne	*splaye that breme*	*border that pasty*
trusshe that chekyn	*syde that haddocke*	*thye that wodcocke*
nubrace that malarde	*tuske that barbell*	*thye all manner of*
unlace that cony	*culpon that troute*	*small byrdes*
dysmembre that heron	*fynne that cheven*	*trauche that sturgyon*
dysplaye that crane	*transsene that ele*	*undertraunche ye purpos*
dysfygure that pecocke	*unjoynt that bytture*	*tayme that crabbe*
tyre that egge	*untache that curlewe*	*barbe that lobster*

And, as the author so nicely puts it, 'Here endeth the goodly termes'.

THE CASTEL OF HELTH

Gathered and made by Syr Thomas Elyot, Knythte, out of the chiefs Authors of Physyke, whereby every manne may knowe the state of his owne body, the preservation of helth and how to instructe well his physytion in syckness that he be not deceyved.

1539

Sir Thomas' book is concerned mainly with medical advice and diet, but some of it also concerns diet in cookery. 'In meat and drink we must consider five [sic] thynges, Subtaunce, Quantitie, Qualitie, Custome, Tyme, Order.'

The author is steeped in the science of his day and many of his ideas display a good deal of sense but were not without pitfalls judged by modern standards. Sir Thomas like his contemporaries had very definite opinions and gave, as they all did, long lists of foods with their benefits and disadvantages, as well as giving methods of cooking and eating. In company with them, and following Galen, he had no great regard for the virtues of fruits, with the exception of oranges, of which he wrote 'the ryndes taken in a lytell quantitie doo comforteth the stomacke, where it digesteth, specially condite with sugar and taken fastynge in a small quantitie'.

He also gives a list of foods making 'good juyce, ill juyce, ingendrynge choler, fleaume, melancholy, making thick juyce, do hurte the teeth, do hurte the eyes, makes great oppilations, inflatyinge or wyndy. Thynges good for the head, the harte, the liver, the lunges, the eies, the stomacke.'

Here are some of his observations on foods and how they should be treated:

FRUITS, VEGETABLES AND NUTS
Fylberds and hasylnuttes good roasted and eaten with pepper.

Almonds. Five or six of them eaten afore meate, kepe a manne from beyinge drunke; they be hot and moist in the first degree.

Chestyns. They beinge rosted under the ymbers or hot asshes, doo nourysshe the bodye strongely, and eaten with hony fastynge, do helpe the manne of the cowghe.

Capers. Capers styreth appetite, beyinge eaten with otimell, before any other meate.

Orenges. The juyce of orenges, havynge a toste of bredde put into it, with a lyttel powder of myntes, sugar, and a lytell cynamome maketh a very good sauce to provoke appetite.

Lettyse. Among all herbes, none hath soo good juyce as letise . . . it increaseth mylke in a woman's breastes, but abatheth carnall appetite.

Persley is very convenient to the stomache, and comforteth appetite, and maketh the breath sweeter. . . .

Anyseseede maketh swete breathe.

Beans. They make wynde, howe so ever they be ordered . . . byt yf onyons be sodden (boiled) with them, they be less noyfull (harmful).

Turnepes boiled 'nourysheth moch, augmenteth the sede of man, provoketh carnall lust. Easten rawe they stop the appetite.'

Onyons beying eaten in great abundance with meate, they cause one to sleape soundly.

Sage is said to increase fertility in women.

Bourage maketh one mery eaten rawe before meales, or layde in wyne that is drunke.

Rosemary has many virtues including helping a cough if taken with pepper and honey.

FLESSHE
The author gives special notes for Englishmen: 'Here in England, grosse meates may be eaten in a great quantitie; and in a cholerick stomake biefe is better digested than a chykens legge'. Or 'Befe of Englande to Englyshemen whiche are in helthe, bryngeth stronge nouryshynge, but it maketh grosse bloudde, and ingendereth melancholy; but being of yonge oxen, not excedynge the age of foure yeares, to them which have cholerike stomakes, it is more convenient, thanne chykens, and other lyke meates'.

Of mutton, he writes, 'Galene doth not commende it, not withstanding experience proveth here in this realme, that if it be yonge, it is a ryght temperate meate'.

Of 'byrdes', he writes that the best are those 'whiche truste most to their wynges, and do brede in hygh countreyes', while he says the capon 'is above al other foules praysed for as much as it is easily digested', adding, 'Hennes in wynger are almost equal unto the capon, but they do not make so stronge nourishment. Aucien saythe yf they be rosted in the bealy of a kydde or lambe, they wyl be better.'

The author describes the parts of beasts as follows: innards, gysar, lyver, trypes, chitterlynges, lunges, lyghtes, splene or mylte, harte, brayne, marowe, stones and udders, heed, tongue and feet.

FISH
He quotes Galen, saying the best fish were sea fish 'the more calme that the water is, the warse is the fyshe'.

EGGS
He recommends eggs, especially if newly laid. 'If they be harde, they be slowe in digestion; but beynge ones digested, they do nowryshe moche. Mean between rere and hard, the dygeste conveniently, and nouryshe quykely. Egges well poched are better than roasted. If they be fryed harde, they be yll nouryshement. They be most holsome, whan they be poched and most unholsome when they be fryed'.

DYETS DRY DINNER
by Henry Buttes Master of Artes and Fellow of the C.C.C. in C
1599

A delightful little book devoted to the uses of fruits, herbs, meat and fish, as well as spices, sauces and, curiously, tobacco. Its main charm lies in its ingenuous 'Table Talk'. One side of each page is given to subject matter, and the opposite to the so-called table talk. There is but one item to each page. In his introduction, Buttes mentions different diets for different localities.

Norfolkmen. For they are true Catholiques in matter of Dyet.... Here are Lettuces for every mans lips.

For the Northern-man, white-meates, Beefe, Mutton, Venison.

For the Southerne man, Fruites, Hearves, Fowle, Fish, Spice and Sauce.

As for Middlesex or Londoner, I smell his diet. Here is a pipe of right Trinidado for him.

The Yorkers, they will bee content with bald Tabacodocko. What should I say?

Here is good Veale for the Essex-man, passing Leekes and excellent cheese for the Welshman . . . here are neither Eg-pyes for the Lancashire man, nor wag-tayles for the Kentish man.

Buttes' methods of cooking are in general a repetition of the cooking of his fellow cookery book writers. But we might easily take his advice concerning the eating of peaches: 'Eate them alwaies fasting, and drink a cup of the best wine, most fragrant and well aromatized.'

Translate this into a sun-ripened peach and a glass of chilled Sauternes and we have the best of ye olde and the new world.

HONNY

CHOICE Pure, most splendant: whitest: curdled and thicke.

USE It healeth the stomack, therefor wholesome for old folkes: dispoleth to the ftowle: refirleth putrefaction: makes good blood.

HURT Worst for hot stomackes, enflaming the blood, and through this acrimony, increaseth choller.

CORRECTION Eate it with fruit, sower meats, or with saccarum Rosatum.

DEGREE Hot and drie in the second.

SEASON [sic]

AGE [sic]

CONSTITUTION In winter, for old, cold and reumaticke.

MEL (honey)
Storie for Table-Talke

'All honny is made of Dewe. For out of flowers the Bees gather that which they make their Combes: of the gum which droppeth from trees, they make waxe: of Dewe they make Honny. So that Dewe is congealed together and crassified either by liuing creatures, and is made Honny: or of it owne accord, which also is Honny, usually tearmed Dry Manna: or is not thickened at all, which they call liquid Manna. Whereof there is great store about Hormus, a Cittie in Arabia Felix.'

TABLE TALK ON PEACOCK

'Peacocke, is very hard meate, of bad temperature, and as euil juyce. Wonderously increaseth melancholy and casteth (as it were) a clowd upon the minde. It layeth at the third yeare, and liueth five and tentie. It is so spitefull and enuious, that it eateth his owne dung, least anybody should make any use of it.

'Great Alexander, imposed a great penaltie on him that killed a Peacocke.'

VITULINA (Veal)
Storie for Table Talk

'The Italians should be calfes by their name; for Italos in Greeke is the same that Vitulus in Latin, and calfe in English. Therefore they collaude it by tearming it Vitella, *id est vitamillia dans*: signifying the holesomenesse thereof to a good stomacke. It is good for sound and able constitutions, not so good for the weake, sicke or languishing stomackes, for it is of a lash and yet grosse substance, not very digestible. Essex calfes the prouerb praiseth, and some are of the minde that Waltcombe Calfe was also that countrey man.'

LACTUCA (Lettuce)
Storie for Table Talk

'Galen commendeth Lettuce thus: in a young man, it abateth the burning heat of his stomach: unto an old man it causeth sleepe. In olde time they ate Lettuce after supper, to represse vapors arising from the stomack to the braine, and to dispose them selves to sleepe. For they used to dine very sparingly, but supped largely.

'Arsitxenes Cyraenaeus watred his Lettuces with Mead, to make them bigger and sweeter.

'*Lactuca a lacta quasi Lactoca* because it breeds milk in women saith Martiall.'

PETROSELINUM (Parsley)
Stories for a Table Talk

'The excellency of this hearb, accordeth with the frequent use thereof. For there is almost no meate or sauce which will not have Perseley either in it or about it. Our English word Persley, is a manifest contract of the Latin *Petroselinum*.

'The chiefest vertue lieth in the roote: second in the seed: last and least in the leauves and yet these are of most use in the kitching.'

VIA RECTA AD VITAM LONGAM

by Dr Tobias Venner
Doctor of Physicke in Bathe

1620

Dr Tobias Venner, a man of decided views, was born in 1577. He was a practising physician and his book, addressed to rural people of high and low estate, is packed with homely advice. One of his firm beliefs was that two meals daily were enough for anyone except the very young, the aged and the infirm. He disapproved of 'bull's beefe' as being 'of a ranke and unpleasant flavour', but he thought it all right for the 'poore hard labourer' to eat. Since 'poore hard labourers' were almost entirely carnivorous and ate almost anything they could get, 'bull's beefe' was probably one of the least of their dislikes.

The good doctor also disapproved of 'fysshe', the eating of which he considered caused a number of diseases, including 'the gout, the stone, the leaprie and the scurvie', and many other skin botherations of an even worse nature.

Pigeons he pronounced 'bread an inflamed bloud and stimulate carnall lust', whilst 'hare's flesh breedeth melancholy'.

Water, the doctor felt, was a pleasant enough drink for people in the tropics but not for an Englishman. He approved of alcohol but not when drunk in excess. 'Drunkards', he declared, were subject to many 'Crapulentall hurts.'

He was also the first English writer on food and drink to state his disapproval of smoking between courses at a meal, and he wrote of this unpleasant habit in his *Briefe and Accurate Treatise Concerning the taking of the Fume of Tobacco* (1621).

Well, doubtless Dr Venner practised what he preached, for when he died in 1660 he had outlived two wives and all his children. A second and third edition of his book appeared in 1622 and 1628 respectively with a splendid introduction by the author himself.

THE CLOSET OF
THE EMINENTLY LEARNED
SIR KENELME DIGBIE KT. OPENED

1669

There were few more interesting personalities of the seventeenth century than the flamboyant Sir Kenelme Digbie. He was knighted by his king, and was known as the 'ornament of England', 'the wonder of the age', and 'the matchless Digbie'. He was poet, diplomat, chemist, physician, philosopher, student of the occult, and amateur collector of cookery recipes wherever he travelled.

Digbie travelled partly for pleasure, sometimes for work, and also while he was in exile. He was a favourite with the Stuarts, clapped into prison by the Long Parliament, bailed out at the intervention of the Dowager Queen Mother of France and sent into exile with his estates confiscated. However, he seems to have corresponded a great deal with Oliver Cromwell on the subject of fair play to the Catholics, and also on the new science of physics in which both men were interested. It would even seem that through correspondence the two men became friends. With the restoration of the monarchy and the Stuarts, Digbie returned to England where he died at the age of sixty-two.

His book was printed in 1669 by the permission of his son, John Digbie. It includes recipes from his life-long collection and, as one writer says, it reads at times like a social register. Sir Kenelme offers 'white metheglin of My Lady Hungerford', which is greatly praised. We have also 'The Queen Mother's Hotchpot of Mutton'; 'My Lord d'Aubigny eats Red herrings thus broyled', or 'My Lady of Newport bakes her Venison in a dish thus'.

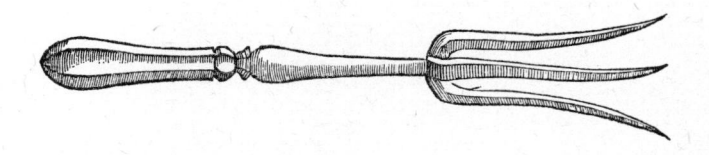

These recipes give us some idea of the richness of the Stuart eating, and we are not surprised that the Stuarts perpetuated the royal tradition of dying of a surfeit of this or that, of the stone, intestinal torments, the agues etc. Sir Kenelme, like most of the people of his time, wrote mostly of meat dishes; vegetables, he believed with the rest of his contempories, gave the wind, milk was choleric, and butter was fit solely for the poor. Only an odd custard was offered to counteract the richness of the Sir Kenelme Digbie style of feeding.

Many of the recipes are impossible or even repellent by today's standards. Sir Kenelme offers us a drink called 'Cock's Ale' in which a cock is boiled, then pounded in a mortar with stoned raisins, dates, spices and sack, 'and when the Ale hath done working, put these in and stop it close six or seven days, and then bottle it, and a month after you may drink it'. This must have been heavy in the extreme.

Probably the language of Sir Kenelme's book is more than half its charm. He does not instruct his cook to add the raisins but to sprinkle in 'the best blue-raisins of the sun' and do the sprinkling with ceremony. He does not say 'bake for 20 minutes in the oven' as we so prosaically do, but by 'an Ave Maria while', or for as long as 'your pulse beateth 200 strokes'. A dish is left to thicken 'till you may see your shadow in it', while tea is brewed 'by the saying of the Miserere Psalm leisurely'.

Here also are two splendid examples of Sir Kenelme Digbie's cooking. A roast of beef took several hours of marinating and much dressing and cooking before it reached the table. Into its preparation went the best full-bodied claret, sweet herbs and all the usual spices of the period, as well as oysters, mushrooms, chestnuts, pistachios, and finally toasted bread. It should have been good.

One wonders for how many Sir Kenelme was baking when a cake demanded eight quarts of flour, one quart of cream, five pounds of butter, one pound of loaf sugar and a quart of ale yeast – plus rosewater and twelve pounds of currants. That this monstrosity was baked in a hot brick oven for only two hours causes some wonder.

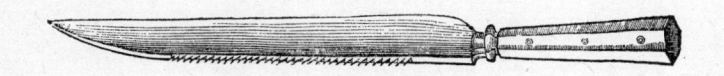

What a world it was indeed! Anne Macdonell, who edited the book in 1910, wrote of it: 'It is a curious old world we get a glimpse of, at once barbarous, simple, and extravagant, when great ladies were expected to see to the milking of the cows as closely as Joan Cromwell supervised her milch kine (milk cows) in St James's Park, and to the cleanliness of their servants' arms and hands, and when huntsmen rode at the bidding of the cook, "for in order that venison be in good condition", before the deer be killed he ought to be hunted and chased as much as possible'.

Sir Kenelme had much to say on the subject of drink. He believed in mead and metheglin as drinks for the young and old. Introducing one particular mead recipe, he wrote: 'this mead is singularly good for consumption, stone, gravel, weak sight and many more things. A chief burgomaster of Antwerp used for many years to drink no other drink but this ... and though he were an old man, he was exceedingly vigorous in every way, and had every year a child, had always a good appetite, and a good digestion, and yet was not fat.'

Digbie also was partial to beer and ale, cider and hydromel. Some of the local ales of his day had curious names, indicative doubtless of their strength, 'huff-cap', 'stride-wide', 'father whoreson', 'mad-dog' and 'angel's milk'. He talks of the wines from Spain and the Canaries increasing in popularity, and of a crude gin called *aqua vitae*, fortunately too expensive for most people.

Meals were served in inns, washed down by ale to whet the appetite.

Olde Receipts

The understanding of ancient receipts presents difficulties for the modern cook, although when the terminology is sorted out they make fascinating reading. One is sometimes staggered at the number of eggs called for in a recipe until one realizes it is a bald statement of quantity and not of a specific egg: hens were smaller in those days and presumably correspondingly so were their eggs. Pigeon's eggs were also used and so a recipe calling for a dozen or more eggs was not quite as extravagant as it might sound.

Recipes for the rare fish and meat jellies, or those calling for porpoise, heron, puffin or whale etc., have been omitted from the following recipes for several reasons. Generally, in England at least, it is not easy to go into a store and buy a pound or so of porpoise, puffin or even whale. Some of the old receipts sound pretty nasty or are untranslatable. Not many people today would like to cook with gum tragacanth or musk. Nor have the rich and somewhat stodgy dishes been included for obvious reasons. Some recipes sound as if they could finish up either as a dish of fish or a sweet pudding. Frequently the recipes tried out for this book produced dishes of remarkable similarity, all saffron yellow, and many of them a hash of some sort.

How then have the recipes been chosen?

Some because they are amusing, others because they are unusual or interesting, many because they are delicious, and finally some because they fall into the simple recipe class.

Our old recipe makers were not in the slightest troubled with accuracy, spelling, consistency or the measurement of ingredients. Nor did they go into detail about baking times or giving exact temperatures. 'Have a care not too bake it too much'; or nicely, 'Let them rest a fair long way – the time it take to walk a furlong'. Also we are told 'to cook it leisurely', and make a 'roll as big as your thumb'. In one recipe we find cherry spelt Cheryrse, Chiryse and Cheweryes.

Many cookery terms and names used in culinary processes before the seventeenth century have become obsolete, and therefore it is important that anyone wanting to make a study of old English recipes should consult the glossary which also makes fascinating reading. Only where necessary have the recipes been translated into the modern idiom. However, for those to whom cooking is fun and an experience, it is worth trying out old recipes in modern kitchens with the mixer or the liquidizer doing in seconds the work that centuries ago demanded an hour or more of hard beating by hand.

BREWET OF AYREN (*The Forme of Cury, circa* 1390)

Take ayren, water, and butter, and seeth him yfere (together), with safron, and gobettes of chese. Wring ayren through a strayner. When the water hath soden (boiled) awhile, takem thene ayren, and swyng hem with verjous and cast therto. Set it over the fire, and let it not boile and serve it forth.

EGG AND CHEESE SOUP

This is similar to the Italian *stracciatella*.

2 pints clear chicken stock, 1–2 eggs, slightly beaten, 2 oz. strong cheese, diced, salt, pepper to taste.

Bring the stock to the boil, stir in the eggs and cheese, season well, bring almost to the boil and stir with a fork for 1–2 minutes. Serve at once.

DRAWEN BEANS Green Bean Soup (*The Forme of Cury, circa* 1390)
Translated from Middle English

Green beans, onions, salt, pepper, stock, sherry.

This recipe leaves all quantities entirely to the cook. Prepare as many green beans as required in the usual manner, put them into a pan with plenty of water, add finely chopped onion to taste, and season generously. Bring this to the boil and continue cooking until the beans are soft. Add stock as required, and sherry to taste, reheat and serve the soup hot with sippets.

This makes a good soup of splendid colour and a change from green pea soup. Recommended as a dish for the poor.

FUNGES (*The Forme of Cury, circa* 1390)

Take funges, and pare hem clene, and dyce hem; take leke, and shred hem small, and do hym to seeth in gode broth; colour it with safron, and do thereinne powder-fort.

This is simple enough. Take as many mushrooms as required, clean, pare and cut into small pieces. Put into a pan with shredded leek and plenty of good broth. Colour and flavour with saffron and add spices to taste.

MUSHROOM SOUP

This is so much nicer than opening a can. One pound of mushrooms with 1 leek is a generous measurement, plus 2 pints or a little more of broth. The saffron should only be a pinch and first soaked in a little water – the spices (powder-fort) could be nutmeg and mace.

FOR EGGES

Take some Egges and beat them well with a little faire water and salt, then take a frying pan and melt your Butter: and then put in your Egges, then take a knife and lift up your Egges, that the raw may goe all to the bottom of the pan, then turne it up with your knife on every side that it may become square, then lay a dish upon the pan, and then turne the pan upside down upon the dish and so serue in your Egges with Veriuyce and Vinegar, which you will.

This is simply an omelette sprinkled with verjuice or vinegar. Why it should have to be square is not quite clear since it is not easy to make a square omelette.

SOD EGGES

Seeth your Egs almost hard, then peele them, and cut them in quarters, then take a little Butter in a frying pan, and melt it a little browne, then put it in a pan a little vinegar, mustard, pepper and salt, and then put it in a platter upon your egges.

HARD-BOILED EGGS

This is a dish of hard-boiled eggs, peeled and quartered and served in a butter sauce.

4 eggs, hard-boiled, 2 oz. butter, 1 teaspoon dry mustard, 4 teaspoons vinegar, salt, pepper to taste.

Use preferably a wine vinegar or a mixture of tarragon and garlic vinegars. The sauce can also be flavoured with anchovies or capers. A pleasing dish, suitable for a starter to a luncheon or to be eaten as a light snack.

AN AMULET OF GREEN BEANS

Blanch your Beans, and fry them in Butter, with a little Parsley and Chibbol:

That done, pour out the Butter, and put in some Cream, season them well, and let them simmer over a gentle Fire. In the meanwhile, an Amulet is to be made with new-laid Eggs and Cream, and salted at Discretion: When it is enough, dress it on a Dish, thicken the Beans with one or two yolks, and turn them on your Amulet, so as all may be serv'd up hot.

Amulets of the like Nature may be made of Mushrooms, Truffles, Green Pease, Asparagus, Artichoke-Bottoms, Spinach, Sorrel, etc. all being first cut into small Pieces, or shred fine.

The name omelette, according to some authorities, is a derivation of *amelette*, meaning blade, transposed through the usual distortions of time, including *alemette* and *alumette*. As usual the early English cookery book writers had their own versions of the spellings. Amulet, amelet, aumlet, and recipes for this many-named dish of eggs often called for as many as 25 eggs; but no one specified what size of egg or what kind. Since the above recipe does not specify any quantities at all, it is a matter of using one's common sense.

TO MAKE BUTTERED EGGES

Take eight yolkes of egges, and put them into a pint of creame, beat them together and straine them into a possenet all, setting upon the fire and stirring it, and let it seeth until it quaile, then take it and put it into a clean cloth, and let it hang so that the Waye may auoide from it, and when it is gone beate it into a dishe of rosewater and suger, with a spoon, and so you haue fine butter. This don, you may take the white of the same eggs putting it into another pint of cream, using it as the yolkes were used, and thus you may haue as fine white butter as you haue yellow butter.

TO MAKE A SALLET OF ALL KIND OF HEARBES

Take your hearbes and picke them very fine into faire water, and picke your flowers by themselues, and washe them al cleane, and swing them in a strainer, and when you put them into a dish, mingle them with Cowcumbers or Lemons payred and sliced, and scrape Suger, and put in Vinegar and Oyle, and throwe the flowers on the toppe of the sallet, and of euery sorte of the aforesaide things, and garnish the dish about with the foresaide things, and harde Egges boyled and laide about dish and upon the sallet.

TO MAKE A GRAND SALLET (*The Second Book of Cookery*, 1641)

Take the buds of al kind of good Hearbs and a handfull of French Capers, seven or eight Dates cut in long slices, a handfull of Raisins of the Sun, the stones being pickt out, a handfull of Almonds blancht, a handfull of Curans, five or six Figs sliced, a preserued orenge cut in slices: mingle al these together with a handful of Sugar, then take a faire Dish fit for a shoulder of Mutton, set a standard of paste in the midst of it, put your aforesaid sallet about this standard, set upon your sallet foure half Lemmons, with the flat ends downward, right over against one another, halfe way betwixt your standard and the dishes side, pricke in every one of these Lemmons a branch of Rosemary and hang upon the Rosemary preserued cherries, or cherries fresh from the tree: set foure half Egges, being roasted hart, betwaene your Lemons, the flat ends downward, prick upon your Egges sliced Dates and Almonds: then you may lay another garnish betweene the brim of the Dish and the Sallet, of quarters of hard Egges and round slices of Lemmons: then you may garnish up the brim of the Dish with a preserued Orenge, in long slices and betwixt every slice of orenge, a little heap of French Capers. If you have not a standard to serue it in, then take halfe a Lemmon, and a faire branch of Rosemary.

SAWSE NOYRE FOR CAPONS YROSTED (*The Forme of Cury, circa* 1390)

Take the lyver of capons, and roost it wele. Take anyse (aniseed) and greynes de Paris (cardamom), gynger, canel (cinnamon), and a lytill crust of brede, and grinde it smale: and grynde it up with verjous and with grece of capons. Boyle it and serve it forth.

DARK SAUCE

This is a liver pâté type of sauce. The following is an approximate modern version of the Middle English.

1 oz. chicken fat, ½ lb. chicken livers, a little ground aniseed, cinnamon, ground ginger and cardamom, 1 small crust of bread, brandy and a little stock.

Heat the fat, add the livers and fry until tender. Mix the spices with the bread crust. Combine with the livers and mince it finely or, better still, put it in a blender. Add brandy and enough stock to make the mixture into a sauce of medium thickness, bring gently to the boil and serve with roast capon or chicken.

SAWSE SARZYNE (*The Forme of Cury, circa* 1390)

Take heppes (hips) and make hem clene. Take almonds blanched. Frye hem in oile, and bray hem in a mortar, with heppes. Drawe it up with rede wyne, and do therinne sugar ynowhg (enough), with powdor-fort. Lat it be stondyng (stiff) and alay it with floer of rys, and color it with alkenet, and messe it forth, and florish it with pome garnet (pomegranates). If thou wilt, in fleshe day, seeth capons, and take the brawne, and tese hem smal, and do (put) therto, and make the lico (liquid of this broth).

Saracen Sauce
1 oz. blanched almonds, a little sweet oil or butter, 10 tablespoons rose hip syrup, 4 tablespoons red wine, 1 dessertspoon ground rice or cornflour, cinnamon to taste, pomegranate seeds to garnish.

Chop the almonds and lightly fry in oil or butter. Combine the syrup, wine and ground rice. Pour into a small pan and cook until the mixture is thick. Add the almonds and cinnamon and garnish with pomegranate seeds.

This sauce may be served with cream, and also with meat such as venison. It is a deep red colour when cooked. Sugar is not needed if using rose hip syrup, nor is alkanet or other red colouring. The flavouring of the sauce is excellent.

FINE SAUCE FOR A ROASTED RABBIT USED TO KING HENRIE THE EIGHTH (*The Treasure of Commodious Conceits and Hidden Secretes, Commonly Called the Good Huswives Closet*, 1591)

Take a handful of washed Parcelie, mince it small, boyle it with Butter and Verjuice uppon a Chafingdish, season it with Sugar, and a little Pepper grose beaten: When it is ready, put in a few crummes of white bread amongst the other; let it boile againe, till it be thicke: then lay it in a platter, like the breadth of three fingers, lay of each side one roasted conie, or mow, and to serve them.

Parsley Bread King Henry's Sauce
This is a sauce which marries just as well with chicken or lamb as with rabbit.

Chop a large bunch of parsley (and a really large bunch) finely. Heat enough butter to fry until it is a light brown. Add a little lemon juice (this is a matter of taste), salt and pepper, and just enough soft breadcrumbs to thicken the sauce. Bring this all to the boil. It can be served hot or cold.

King Henry's sauce makes a pleasant change from onion or mint sauce with lamb.

TO PICKLE MACKREL, CALLED CAVEACH (*The Lady's Companion*, 1733)

Cut your Mackrel into round Pieces, and divide one into five or six Pieces: To fix large Mackrel you may take one Ounce of Beaten Pepper, three large Nutmegs, a little Mace, and a Handful of Salt; mix your Salt and beaten spice together, and make two or three Holes in each Piece, and thrust the

Seasoning into those Holes with your Fingers; rub the Pieces all over with the Seasoning; fry them brown in Oil, and let them stand till they are dry; then put them into Vinegar, and cover them with Oil. They will keep well covered a great while, and are very delicious.

SOALS TO DRESS FINELY FRYED (*The Family Dictionary, or Houshold Comepanion,* by William Salmon)

Take a pair of large Soals and flay them on both sides: then fry them in sweet Suet, tied up with Spice, Bay-leaves, and Salte, then lay them into a Dish, and put into them some Butter, Claret-Wine, and two Anchovies, cover them with another, set them over a Chaffing-Dish of Coals, and let them stew awhile; then serve them to the Table, garnish your Dish with Orange or Limon, and Squeeze some over them.

Fried and Dressed Sole (Translation)
This recipe can be done almost as well with plaice or haddock fillets – it does a lot for the latter which are firm enough to take the extra cooking. Instead of taking the fish out of the pan and placing them on a chafing dish (although there is nothing against this), the fat can be poured off and the butter, claret etc. added. The pan is then covered and the fish cooked gently in the claret, spices etc. The oranges and lemon should be served in thick slices or wedges and some of their juice squeezed over the fish. This is an excellent dish.

CHYKENS IN HOCCHEE

Take chykens and scald them, take parsel and sawge, without any other erbes, take garlec and grapes, and stoppe the chikens ful, and seeth them in good broth, so that they may esely be boyled thereinne. Messe them and cast thereto powdor-douce.

Boiled and Stuffed Chicken
Take chickens and fill them with parsley and sage (no other herbs), garlic and grapes. Boil them in broth, serve and sprinkle lightly with cinnamon and sugar.
   It is important to completely close the openings of the chickens after stuffing them to prevent the stuffing from falling out.
   An interesting combination.

FARSURE FOR CHICKINS (*Egg Stuffing for Chicken*)
Modernized version only.

3 yolks hard-boiled eggs, a large bunch parsley, 1 oz. currants, $\frac{1}{2}$ teaspoon mixed spice, $\frac{1}{2}$ oz. fat (lard, butter or margarine), beaten egg to bind.

Mix all together and stuff into the bird at the start of cooking. This is enough for a small chicken.

TO FARCE ALL SORTS OF FOWL (*The Queen's Closet Opened or The Pearl of Practise,* 1656)

Take Veal-Sweet-Breads, oisters, Anchovies, Marrow, a few Chives, a little Thyme, Savoury and Marjoram, with some Lemmen-Peel, Salt, Pepper and Nutmeg. All these being well temper'd with the Yolk of an Egg, raise up the skin on the Breast of your Fowls, stuff it, and stick it up again: Then fill their Bellies with oisters, roast them and let them, be served up with strong Gravy-Sauce.

BEEF FLAMODE (*The Family Dictionary, or Houshold Companion,* by William Salmon)

To make the best way: Take of the Fillet of Beef and the lean of Pork, shred them together and season it; then take Bacon and cut it into big Lardons, rowl them in Pepper and Salt, and lay them between the meat in the Stew-pan and let it stew easily in its own Broth, and it will be exceeding short and tender; and will tast like Venison. You may also make an excellent Pye or Pasty of this: putting butter upon it.

This dish should be cooked over a low heat – the bacon or lardons should be placed in layers with the meat – and quantities are all for us to use as we wish. It is pleasant and the meat combination unusual.

TO MAKE STEWED STEAKES (*The Good Huswifes Jewell,* by Thomas Dawson, 1596)

Take a peece of Mutton, and cutte it in pieces, and wash it very cleane, and put it in a faire potte with Ale, or with halfe Wine, then make it boyle, and skumme it cleyne, and put into your pot a faggot of Rosemary and Time, then some parsely picked fine, and some onyons cut round, and let them all boyle together, then take prunes, and raisons, dates and currans, and let it boyle altogether, and season it with Sinamon and Ginger, Nutmeggs, two or three Cloues, and Salt, and so serue it on soppes and garnish it with fruite.

MUTTON: A LEG ROASTED WITH OYSTERS (*The Family Dictionary, or Houshold Companion,* by William Salmon)

Take a large Leg of Mutton, and stuff it well with Mutton Suet, Pepper, Nutmeg, Salt and Meal, then roast it and stick it with Cloves when it is half roasted, cut off some of the under-side of the fleshy end in little thin bits then take a Pint of Oysters, and the Liquor of them, a little Mace, sweet-butter and Salt, put all these with the bits of Mutton in a Pipkin, till half be consumed, then dish your Mutton and pour this Sauce over it, strew Salt about the Dish side and serve it in.

This is, in fact, a simple dish, the mutton can be larded if necessary instead of being stuffed, and the spices well rubbed into the flesh. Whether or not the cloves go in when the meat is half roasted is a matter of taste; but do not add more than two, for cloves are strong in flavour. When the meat is half cooked, take it from the oven, remove the fatty fleshy bits, and return for further cooking. From this point the author's explanations are adequate for all readers without further explanation.

Another pleasant dish and for us today with our all too usual mint sauce, excellent.

LUMBER-PYE (*The Queen's Closet Opened or The Pearl of Practise*, 1656)

Let the umbles of a Deer be parboil'd and well clear'd from the Fat; then put to them as much Beef-suet as Meat or more and chop all together very fine: To these add three or four pounds of Currans, half a Pound of Sugar, a pint of Sact, a little Rose-water, half a Pound of Candy'd Orange, Lemmon and Citron-peel, Dates stoned and stic'd with Cloves, Mace, Cinnamon, Nutmeg, and a little Salt. Having fill'd your Pye, close it; and when 'tis bak'd, pour in somewhat above half a pint of Canary-Wine.

SALMOGUNDY (*The Lady's Companion*, 1733)

Recipes as well as spelling vary for this old English supper dish.

Mince very fine two boiled or roasted Chickens, or Veal, which you like best: Mince also very small the Yolks and the Whites of hard Eggs by themselves: Shred also the Pulp of a Lemon very small: then lay in the Dish a Layer of minced Meat, a Layer of the Yolks, and then a Layer of the Whites of Eggs, over which a Layer of Anchovies, and on them a Layer of the shred Pulp of a Lemon, next a Layer of Pickles minced small, then a Layer of Sorrel, and last of all a Layer of Spinach and Onions, or Shallots, shred small: Having thus filled the Dish, set an Orange or Lemon on the Top, and garnish with scraped Horse-radish, Barberries, and Slices of Lemon; let the sauce be Oil, beat up thick, with the Juice of Lemons, Salt, and Mustard. We serve this Dish, in the second Course, or for a Side-dish, or a Middle-Dish for Supper. You may always make Salmogundy of such Things as you have, according to your Fancy, and in what Forms you like, as a Star, Pyramid, or the Shape of a Herring, putting the Head and Tail of the Herring to it.

TO MAKE FRITTERS OF SPINNEDGE

Take a good deale of Spinnedge, and washe it cleane, then boyle it in faire water, and when it is boyled, then take it forth and let the water runne from it, then chop it with the backe of a knife, and then put it in some egges and grated Bread, and season it with Sugar, Sinamon, Ginger and Pepper, Dates minced fine, and currans, and rowle them like a ball, and dippe them in Batter made of Ale and flower.

These would then have to be fried in deep oil until brown. They are sweet and extremely good. Spinach, like marrow, was used rather more in sweet dishes than in savoury ones.

TO STEW PEASE AFTER THE FRENCH FASHION (*The Lady's Companion*, 1733)

Cut Lettuce into little Bits, and also two or three Onions, take some Butter and Slices of Bacon, season these with Salt and whole Pepper, and toss them up in a Stew-pan till the Lettuce is hot; then put it in a Quart of Pease, and let them stew till they are tender; then add to them some good Broth or boiling Water, and let them stew again gently; broil a Piece of Bacon, and lay in the Middle of the Dish with grated Bread and chopp'd Parsley; pour in your Pease, etc. and serve it up.

PUDDING OF MARROW BAKED (*The Family Dictionary, or Houshold Companion*, by William Salmon)

Let your Dish be indifferent deep, on the bottom whereof, lay Sippets of white Bread, and on that lay raw Marrow all over, with Dates, Raisins of the Sun, Orangado, and other Suckets, then having ready some Cream boil'd up with the Yolks of Eggs, lay thereon a Ladleful or two thereof, Marrow upon that, upon your Marrow make another lay of Dates, Raisins, etc., and then a lay of Cream; continue so doing, till you have fill'd up your Dish, garnish the brim of your Dish with Paste, then set it in the Oven half an Hour, and it will be enough. In the boiling your Cream, you must put in whole Cinamon, and large Mace, and season it with Rosewater, Sugar, and grated Nutmeg.

This is a perfect example of the use of marrow served as a sweet.

SPANISH PAP (*The Queen's Closet Opened or The Pearl of Practise*, 1656)

Take three spoonfuls of Rice-Flower finely beaten and sifted, two yolks of Eggs, three spoonfuls of Sugar and three or four spoonfuls of Rosewater. Temper these four together and put them to a Pint of Cream; then set it on the Fire, and keep it stirred till it come to a reasonable thickness; then Dish it and serve it up.

PAERES IN CONFYT (*The Forme of Cury, circa* 1390)

Take paeres, and pare hem clene. Take gode red wyne, and mulberes, other (or) sandres (*see* Glossary) and seeth the paers therinne. Ane whan thei buth isode (are boiled), take hem up, make a syrup of wyne greke, or vernage, with blanche powdor other (or white sugar), and powder gynger; and do the peres therein. Seeth it a lytel and messe it forth.

Pears Cooked in Red Wine (Translation)
This recipe is similar to the Italian *Pere Cotta*.
6 ripe pears, red wine, 4–6 tablespoons sugar.
Peel the pears, remove the stalk but keep the pears whole. Mix the wine and sugar in a pan, bring gently to the boil, add the pears and bring again to the boil. There must be enough wine to cover the pears. Boil for about 10 minutes or until the pears are tender, basting them with the syrup from time to time.

MRS MEDGATES GOOS-BERRY CUSTARD (*The Ladies Companion,* 1653)

When you have cut off the stucks and Eys of your Goos-berries, and washed them, then boyle them in water till they will break with a spoon, then strain them, and beat half a dozen Eggs and stir them together upon a Chafin-dish of coles with some Rosewater, then sweeten them very well with Sugar, and always serve it cold to the table for a closing-dish.

Mrs Medgate's Cold Gooseberry Custard (Translation)
1 lb. gooseberries, a little water, 6 small eggs, 1 tablespoon rosewater, 4 oz. sugar.
Top and tail the gooseberries, wash them and cook in just enough water to prevent burning until they reach breaking point. Strain off the excess liquid. Beat the eggs with the rosewater, mix into the gooseberries, add the sugar and cook gently until the mixture is thick. Serve cold.

A variety of gooseberry fool. It is best to turn out the custard into glasses or custard cups.

TO MAKE A GOOSEBERRY CUSTARD (*A True Gentlewomans Delight,* by W. J., 1653)

Take as many Gooseberries as you please, boyle them till they be soft, then take them out, and let them stand and cool, and drain them, draw them with your hand through a canvas Strainer, then put in a little Rosewater, Sugar, and three Whites, and stirre them altogether, and put them in a Skillet, and stirre them apace else they will burn, let them stand and cool a little while, and take them off, and put them in a glasse.

Gooseberry Custard
1 lb. gooseberries, 2 tablespoons rosewater, 4 oz. sugar, 4 egg whites, whipped.
Top and tail the gooseberries and cook them in a little water until soft. Take them from the pan, cool and drain off surplus liquid. Rub them through a strainer. Put the gooseberries, the rosewater and sugar into a pan. Lightly whisk the egg whites and stir them into the gooseberries over a gentle heat until the mixture rises in the pan and becomes slightly thick. Let the mixture cool, and serve in glasses.

PORREYNE (prune fool) Modernized version only.

for 4 persons
1 lb. prunes, 4 tablespoons honey, 2 oz. butter, 1 tablespoon cornflour.

Soak the prunes until soft. Stone and mince them (or put through a blender). Mix with the honey, butter and cornflour. Bring gently to the boil and cook until the mixture thickens. The fool can be served hot or cold.

SPANISH CREAM (*The Lady's Companion*, 1733)

Take three Spoonfuls of Rice-flour, sifted very fine, three Yolks of Eggs, three Spoonfuls of Water, and two Spoonfuls of Orange-flower-water; mix them well together, then put to it one Pint of Cream, and set it on a good Fire, keeping it stirring till it is of a good Thickness; afterwards dish it, and keep it cold.

PISTACHOE CREAM AU BAIN MARIE (*The Lady's Companion*, 1733)

Put to a Quart of Cream or Milk, a Bit of Sugar, a Stick of Cinnamon, and a Bit of green Lemon, and let it boil a little; then put in it a Quarter of a Pound of scalded and well pounded Pistachoes: Keep some whole to garnish your Dish. A Quarter of a Pound is but for a small Dish, you must proportion your Quantity to the Size of your Dish, Pour your Cream of Pistachoes through a Sieve into a Dish, with the Yolks of six Eggs, and strain it two or three Times: After this put a Stew-pan full of Water over a Stove, let your Dish be bigger than the Stew-pan, so that the Bottom of it may touch the Water: Then put in your Cream, and cover it with another Dish turned upside down, with some Charcoal over it. This Cream may sometimes be served hot, for a dainty Dish in the second Course.

Instead of cooking this cream on top of the stove, the dish can be put in a slow oven in a pan of water and baked until set. A combination of cream and milk makes a sufficiently rich mixture. The pistachio nuts can be finely ground and then pounded. Double the quantity of pistachio nuts can be used, as they give an excellent flavour.

A BEGGAR'S PUDDING (*The Lady's Companion,* 1733)

Take some stale Bread, pour over it some hot Water, till it is well soak'd; then press out the Water, and mash the Bread; add some powdered Ginger, and Nutmeg grated, a little Salt, some Rose-water or Sack, some Lisbon sugar, and some Currants; mix these well together, and lay it in a Pan well butter'd on the Sides, and when it is well flatted with a Spoon, lay some Pieces of Butter on the Top, bake it in a gentle Oven, and serve it hot, with grated Sugar over it. You may turn it out of the Pan when it is cold, and it will eat like a Cheesecake.

TO MAK PAYN PARDIEU (*A Noble Boke off Cookry ffor a Prynce houssolde or eny other estately Housshoulde.* Reprinted and edited by Mrs Napier in 1882 from a fifteenth-century manuscript in the Holkham Collection.)

To make payn pardieu tak paynmayne or freshe bred and paire away the cruste cut them in schyves and fry them a littill in clarified butter then tak yolkes of eggs drawe throughe a strene as hot as ye may and lay the bred ther in and turn it therin that they be coveryd in better and serve it and straw on sugar enowghe.

Lost Bread (Pain Perdu) (Translation)
8 thick slices fresh white bread, butter for frying, 4 egg yolks, well beaten, sugar.
Cut off the crusts from the bread. Heat enough butter to fry the slices. Fry them lightly in the hot butter. Take from the pan and dip them first in the beaten egg yolks and then fry again in the hot butter, turning to let the slices brown on both sides. Sprinkle with sugar to serve.

TO MAKE A DISH CALLED POOR KNIGHTS (*The Queen's Closet Opened or The Pearl of Practise,* 1656)

Cut two Penny-Loaves into round slices (about six) and dip them in half a Pint of Cream, or fair Water; then lay them abroad in a Dish, and let three Eggs be beaten with Cream, grated Nutmeg and Sugar: That done, melt some Butter in a Frying-pan, wet the sides of the Toasts, and lay them on the wet side; pour in the rest upon them, and fry them; serve them up with Rose-Water, Sugar and Butter.

This recipe can be followed quite easily without specific modernization of the ingredients. To wet the sides of the toast simply means to place the toast in the egg and cream mixture, place it egg-side down in the frying pan and cover with the rest of the egg mixture.

LISBON BISKETS (*The Queen's Closet Opened or The Pearl of Practise*, 1656)

Let the whites of three or four Eggs, be beaten a little with the Yolks, and add thereto as much Powder-Sugar, as you can take up between your fingers, at four or five Times, with four or five spoonfuls of baked Flower, and some Lemmon-peel. When these are all well imbodied together, turn your paste upon a sheet of Paper strewed with Sugar, strew the paste likewise on the top, with some sugar, and set it in an Oven, moderately heated. As soon as the biskets are bak'd they must be cut all at once with the paper underneath, according to the Size and Figure, you would have them to be of, and then the Paper may be gently pared off with a Penknife.

TO MAKE SHREWSBERY CAKES (*A Delightful Daily Exercise for Ladies and Gentlewomen,* by John Murrell, 1621)

Take a quart of very fine flower, eight ounces of fine sugar beaten and cersed, twelve ounces of sweete butter, a Nutmegge grated, two or three spoonefuls of damaske rosewater, worke all these together with your hands as hard as you can for the space of halfe an houre, then roule it in little round Cakes, about the thicknesse of three shillings one upon another, then take a silver Cup or a glasse some foure or three inches over, and cut the cakes in them, then strow some flower upon white papers and lay them upon them, and bake them in an Oven as hotte as for Manchet. Set up your lid till you may tell a hundreth, then you shall see the white, if any of them rise up clam them downe with some cleane thing, and if your Oven be not too hot set up your lid againe, and in a quarter of an houre they wil be baked enough, but in any case take heede your Oven be not too hot, for they must not looke browne but white, and so draw them foorth and lay them one upon another till they bee could, and you may keep them halfe a yeare the new baked are best.

Shrewsbury Cakes (Translation)
There are several recipes for these little shortbread biscuits or cakes. The following, however, approximates the above recipe.

1 lb. flour, ¼ lb. sugar, ¼ lb. unsalted butter, a little grated nutmeg, a little rosewater.
Combine the flour, sugar and butter and work to a stiff paste. Add the spice and rosewater and beat to a stiff dough. Roll out about ⅛-in. thick and cut into rounds. Bake in a moderate oven (350°F.) for 25–30 minutes.

TO MAKE SHORT CAKES (*The Good Huswives Handmaid, circa* 1597)

Take wheat flower of the fairest yee can get, and put it in an earthen pot, and stop it close, and set it in an Oven and bake it, and when it is baked, it will be full of clods, and therefore ye must searce it through a searce: and the flower will have as long baking as a pastie of Venison. When you have doone this, take clowted creame, or els sweete Butter, but creame is better, then take sugar Cloves, Mace and Saffron, and the yolke of an Egge, for one dozen cakes one yolk is enough: then put these aforesaid things together into the cream, and themer them altogether, then put them to your flower and so make your cakes, your paste will be very short, therefore yee must make your cakes very little: when yee bake your cakes, ye must bake them upon papers, after the drawing of a batch of bread.

Short Cakes (Translation)
6 oz. clotted cream or butter, 4 oz. sugar, 1–2 egg yolks, ½ lb. plain flour, pinch ground mace, cloves and saffron.
Mix the cream and sugar together, add the egg yolks and work them well into the cream. When the mixture is blended, add the flour and spices. Work to a firm dough and shape into biscuits. Bake in a moderate oven (350°F.) until a pale beige colour, about 25 minutes.

Eggs and flour vary. If using clotted cream, 1 egg yolk is enough. If using butter, it must first be creamed with the 2 egg yolks before adding the flour and spices.

CREMITARIES or PURSES (*The Good Huswifes Jewell,* 1596)

Take a little Marrow, small raisons and dates, let the stones be taken away, these being beaten together in a Morter, season it with Ginger, Sinamon and Suger, the put it in fine paste, and bake them or frie them, so done in the serving of them cast blaunch powder upon them.

Baked or Fried Turnovers (Translation)
½ lb. puff pastry, a little marrow, diced, 3 oz. raisins or currants, 3 oz. dates, weight after stoning, 1 oz. butter or magarine, 1 dessertspoon sugar, pinch each ground ginger and cinnamon, 1 egg yolk, beaten.

Roll out the pastry and cut into small squares. Combine the remaining ingredients (except the egg) to make a filling. Put a little of this on to each square of pastry, fold over and seal the edges firmly. Make a small hole in the top of each 'purse' or pie. Brush lightly with beaten egg yolk and bake in a hot oven (450°F.) for 20 minutes. Take from the oven and immediately dust with fine sugar. The 'purses' can be fried in deep fat, if preferred.

TO MAKE ALMOND PUFFES (*A Booke of Cookerie – containing many of the best and chosest workes, that are usual at this day, both of French and Dutch fashions. Never before in print till this time.* London 1621.)

Take halfe a pound of blancht Almonds, beate them very fine with a little Rose-water, then mingle them with a quarter of a pound of Sugar, and the whites of two rawe egges, make them in little round cakes setting them upon buttered white Papers, and so bake them, and when you see them beginne to looke white, bake them in an Oven as hot as for Manchet, and when they looke white draw them out and then put them in a dish, then poure upon them Rose-water and Butter, scrape upon the good store of Sugar, and set them into the Oven againe, while they be candied upon the toppe, then draw them foorth, and so serve them to the table hotte.

Almond Biscuits (Translation)
This recipe produces rather chewy lump biscuits similar to the traditional Danish *kransekage* which is served on festive occasions.
2 egg whites, ½ lb. ground almonds, rose-water, 4 oz. granulated sugar, melted butter.
Beat the egg whites until they are easily held to a peak but are not dry. Mix the almonds with a little rose-water and sugar and fold gently into the beaten egg whites. Drop this mixture in teaspoonfuls on to a buttered baking sheet and bake in a moderate oven (350°F.) for 25–30 minutes. Take from the oven, sprinkle lightly with rose-water and melted butter and generously with sugar. Return to the oven and continue baking until the top is candied. Serve hot.

HOW TO MAKE A GOOD MARCHPANE (*A Book of Cookrye*, 1591)

First take a pound of long smal almonds and blanch them in cold water, and drye them as drye as you can, then grinde them small, and put no licour to them but as you must needs to keep them from oyling, and that licour that you put must be rosewater, and in manner as you shall think good, but wet your Pestel therein, when ye have beaten them fine, take halfe a pound of Sugar and more, and see that it be beaten small in pouder, it must be fine sugar then put it to your Almonds and beate them altogether, when they be beaten, take your wafers and cut them compasse round, and of the bignes you will have your Marchpane and then as soone as you can after the tempering of your stuffe, let it be put in your paste, and strike it abroad with a flat stick as even as you can, and pinch yt very stuffe as it were an edge set upon, and then put a paper unde it, and lay burning coles upon the bottom of the basin. To see how it baketh, if it happen to ben too fast in some place, folde papers as broad as the place is, and lay it upon that place, and thus with attending ye shall bake it a little maore than a quarter of an houre, and when it is wel baked, put on your gold and biskets, and stick in Comfits, and so you shall make a good Marchpaine. Or ever that you bake it you must cast on it fine Sugar and Rosewater that will make it look like Ice.

This was one of the specialities of medieval confectionery which featured in almost all the recipe books of our ancestors and appeared on the table amongst the desserts at ceremonial feasts. Marchpane, marchpain, marzipan or *massepain*, the name exists in several spellings throughout Europe. Originally marchpanes were baked on wafers, much decorated and given away as presents on festive occasions. Brought down to our modern level, we have simply the following:

Marzipan
½ lb. ground almonds, 4 oz. caster sugar, 2–3 tablespoons rose-water.
Combine the almonds and sugar and add enough rose-water to make a firm paste. Roll out and cut or press into moulds or shapes. Bake in a moderate oven (350°F.) for about 20 minutes. The marchpane can be decorated with icing or, better still, with gold or silver leaf (available in many Indian shops). It is simply laid on top.

The following four recipes are from *A Book of Fruits and Flowers*, 1653.

A CONSERVE OF ROSES

Take red Rose buds, clip of all the white, bruised, and withered from them, then weigh them out, and taking to every pound of Roses three pound of Sugar, stamp the Roses by themselves very small, putting a little juice of Lemmons or Rose-water to them as they wax dry, when you see the Roses small enough, put the Sugar to them, and beat them together till they be well mingled, then put it up in Gally pots or glasses: in like manner are the Conserverves of Flowers, of Violets, Cowslips, Marigolds, Sage and Sea Boise made.

TO PRESERVE ROSES OR ANY OTHER FLOWERS

Take one pound of Roses, three pound of Sugar, one pint of Rose water, or more, make your Syrupe first, and let it stand till it be cold, then take your Rose leaves (petals), having first clipt off all the white, put them into the cold Syrupe, then cover them and set them on a soft fire, that they may but simper for two or three hours, then while they are hot put them into pots or glasses for your use.

TO PRESERVE MEDLERS

Take the fairest Medlers you can get, but let them not be too ripe, then set on faire water on the fire, and when it boyleth put in your Medlers, and let them boyle till they be somewhat soft, then while they are hot pill them, cut off their crowns, and take out their stones, then take to every pound of Medlers, three quarters of a pound of Sugar, and a quarter of a pint of Rose water, seeth your Syrupe, scumming it clean, then put in your Medlers one by one, the stalks downward, when your Syrupe is somewhat coole then set them on the fire againe, let them boyle softly till the Syrupe be enough, then put in a few Cloves and a little Cinnamon, and so putting them up in pots reserve them for your use.

TO MAKE A TART OF MEDLERS

Take meddlers that be rotten, and stamp them, and set them upon a chafin-dish with coales, and beat in two yolks of Eggs, boyling till it be somewhat thick, then season it with Sugar, Cinnamon, and Ginger, and lay it in paste.

The above recipes can be followed without a translation. *The Book of Fruits and Flowers* is charming, with pretty illustrations of plants alongside the recipes.

The following recipes have been included for the culinary adventurous. They are taken from *A New Booke of Cookerie Set Forth by the observation of a Traveller* (John Murrell), 1615.

FRITTERS ON THE COURT FASHION

Take the curdes of a sacke Posset, the yolkes of five new layd Egges, and the whites of two of them, fine flower, and make thicke batter: cut a Pomewafer (apple) in small pieces: season it with Nutmeg, and a little Pepper, put in a little strong Ale, warme Milke, mingle all together, and put them into Lard, neither too hot nor too colde. If your butter swimme, it is in good temper.

TO MAKE PANCAKES SO CRISPE THAT YOU MAY SET THEM UPRIGHT

Make a dozen or a score of them in a little frying pan, no bigger than a sawcer, and then boyle them in Lard, and they will look as yellow as golde beside the taste.

A SALLET OF ROSE-BUDS AND CLOUE GILLY-FLOWERS

Picke Rosebuds, and put them into a earthen Pipkin, with white wine-vinegar and sugar, so may you use Cowslippes, Violets or Rosemary-flowers.

TO MAKE ALL MANER OF FRUIT TARTES

You must boyle your fruite, whether it be apple, cherrie, peach, damson, peare, Mulberie, or codling, in faire water, and when they be boyled inough, put them into a bowle, and bruse them with a Ladle, and when they be colde, straine them, and put in red wine or claret wine, and so season it with suger, sinamon and ginger.

TO PRESERUE ALL KINDE OF FRUITES, THAT THEY SHALL NOT BREAKE IN THE PRESERUING OF THEM

Take a platter that is playne in the bottome, and lay suger in the bottome, then cherries or any other fruit, and so between euerie rowe you lay, throw suger and set it upon a pots heade, and couer it with a dish, and so let it boyle.

TO MAKE BLEWMANGER

Take to a pint of creame twelve or fifteen yolkes of egges, and straine them into it, and seeth them well euer stirring it with a sticke that is broad at the end but before you seeth it put in suger, and in the seasoning tast of it that you may if neede bee put in more suger, and when it is almost sodden put in a little Rose water that it may taste thereof, and seeth it well till it be thicke, and then straine it againe if it hath neede, or else put it in a fayre Dish and stirre it till it be almost cold, and take the white of all the Egges, and straine them with a pint of creame and seeth that with suger, and in the ende put in rosewater as into the other, and seeth it till it be thicke enough, and then use it as the other, and when ye serue it ye may serue one dish and another of the other in roules, and cast on biskets.

TO MAKE APPLE PUFS

Take a Pomewafer or any other Apple that is not hard, or harsh in taste: mince it small with a dozen or twenty Razins of the Sunne, wet the Apples

[105]

in two Egges, beat them all together with the backe of a knife, or a Spoone. Season them with Nutmeg, Rosewater, Sugar and Ginger: drop them into a Frying-pan with a spoone, fry them like Egges, wring on the juyce of an orenge, or Lemmon and serve them in.

TO MAKE A PUDDING IN A FRYING PAN

Take foure Egges, two spoonfuls of Rosewater, Nutmeg grated, sugar, grated Bread, the quantities of a penny Loafe, halfe a pound of Befe Suit minst fine: work them as stiffe as a Pudding with your hand, and put it in a Frying-pan with sweet Butter, frye it browne, cut it in quarters and serve it hot, eyther at Dinner or supper. If it be on a fasting day leave out the Suit, and the Currens and put in two or three Pomewafers minst small, or any other soft Apple that hath a good relish.

TO MAKE ALMOND BUTTER

Take almondes and blanch them, and beate them in a morter verye small and in the bewting put in a little water, and then be beaten, poure in water into two pots, and put in halfe into one and half into another, and put in sugar, and stirre them still, and let them boyle a good while, then straine it, through a strainer with rose water, and so dish it up.

FOR A CAWDEL (Fifteenth-Century Recipe)

Breke ten egges in cup fulle fayre
Do away wthe white with out diswayre: (doubt)
Thou strene also thou put away
And swynge they yolkes with spone, I thee say;
Then mynge (mix) *hem* (them) *wel with gode ale,*
A cup full large take thou schalle,
Set hit (it) *on fyre, styr hit, I telle,*
Bewar ther with that it never welle (boil)
If thous cast salt ther to, iwys
Thou marres alle, so hav I blis.

Caudle or Cawdel (Translation)
For 1 person   2 egg yolks, 1 dessertspoon sugar, 3 dessertspoons ale.
Beat the eggs until smooth, add the sugar and liquid and pour into the top of a double boiler. Cook over almost boiling water, whisking all the time until the mixture is thick. Serve at once in glasses with wine biscuits.

This is very similar to the Italian *zabaglione*.

CAWDEL FERRY

Take floer of payndemayn (white bread) and gode wyne; and drawe it togyere. Do therto a grete quantie of sugar cypre, or hony clarified; and do therto safronn. Boile it, and whan it is boiled, alye (mix) it up with yolkes of ayren, and do therto salt, and messe it forth, and lay theron sugar and powdor gynger.

Wine Cream (Translation)
A pinch of saffron, 1 tablespoon sifted flour, ½ pint red wine or Marsala, 3 tablespoons clear honey, 2 egg yolks, well beaten, sugar and ground ginger.
Soak the saffron in about 1 tablespoon of water. Mix the flour with the wine to make a smooth paste. Add the honey and blend thoroughly. Put this into a pan and cook until the mixture is thick, add the saffron liquid and stir. Take from the heat and gradually pour this cream into the beaten egg yolks. Beat well and leave to cool. Sprinkle with sugar and ground ginger.

A pleasant adaptation of this cream is to add two extra well-beaten eggs or even whipped cream.

TO MAKE BISKET BREAD (*Country Contentments,* Gervase Markham, 1623)

To make Bisket bread, take a pound of fine flower, and a pound of sugar finely beaten and searsed, and mix them together; Then take eight egges and put foure yolkes and beate them very well together; then strow in your flower and sugar as you are beating of it, by a little at once, it will take very neere an houres beating; then take halfe an ounce of Aniseedes and let them be dried and rubbed very cleane and put them in; then rub your Bisket pans with cold sweet butter as thinne as you can, and so put it in and bake it in an oven: But if you would have thinne cakes, then take fruit dishes and rub them in a like sort with butter, and so bake your cakes on them, and when they are amost bak't, turn them and thrust them downe close with your hand. Some to this Bisket bread will adde a little Creame and a few Coriander seedes cleane rubd, and it is not amisse, but excellent good also.

TO MAKE GINGERBREAD

Take a clarret wine and colour it with townesall, and put in sugar and set it to the fire; then take wheat bread finely grated and sifted, and licoras, Aniseeds, Ginger and Cinamon beaten very small and searsed; and put your bread and your spice altogether, and put them into the wine, and boil it and stirre it till it be thicke; then mould it and print at your pleasure, and let it stand neither too moist not too warme.

COARSE GINGER BREAD (*Country Contentments,* Gervase Markham, 1623)

Take a quart of Honie clarified, and seeth it till it bee browne, and if it be thicke, put to it a dish of water; then take fine crummes of white bread grated and put to it, and stirre it well, and when it is almost cold, put to it the powder of Ginger, Cloves and Cinnamon and a little Licoras and Aniseeds: then knead it and put it in moulds and print it: some use to put it also a little Pepper, but that is according unto taste and pleasure.

The following recipes are from *Ancient Cookery* in the British Museum.

CRYSPELS

Take and make a foile (crust) of good past as thynne as paper. Kerve it out and fry it in oile, other (or) in the grece; and the remnant take hony clarified, and flaunne (custard) therewith, alye (mix) hem up, and serve hem forth.

Crisp Cakes
4 egg whites, beaten, 4 tablespoons flour, 3 tablespoons honey, oil and butter for frying, sugar, cream.
Beat the egg whites, fold in the flour and honey and beat to a batter. Heat a very little oil and butter in a pan. Drop the batter into the pan in tablespoonfuls and fry until a golden brown on both sides. Sprinkle with sugar and serve with cream.

TO MAKE A TART OF DAMSONS

Take Damsons and boyle them in wine, eyther red or claret, and put therto a dosin of peares, or els white bread to make them stiff withall, then draw (mix) them up with the yolkes of six Egges, and swete butter and bake it.

TO MAKE A TART OF CHERIES

Take all thinge that ye do to the Tart of damsons, so ye put no peres therto.

TO MAKE A TART OF BOURAGE FLOWERS

Take Bourage flowers and parboile them tender, then strayne them with the yolkes of three or foure egges and sweete curdes, or els take three or fouer apples, and parboyle withall, and strain them with sweete butter, and a little Mace, and so bake it.

TO MAKE A TART OF MARYGOLDES, PRIMROSES OR COUSLIPS

Take the same stuffe to euery of the that you doe to the Tarte of Bourage and the same seasoning.

TO MAKE A TART OF STRAWBERRIES

Take and strain them with the yolke of foure Egges, and a little white bread grated, then season it up with Suger, and swete butter, and so bake it.

TO MAKE A STEWE AFTER THE GUYSE OF BEYONDE THE SEA

Take a potte of faire water, and as much wine, and a brest of mutton chopt in pieces, then set it on the fier, and scom it cleane, and put thereto a dishe full of sliced onyons, and a quantity of cinnamon, ginger, cloues, and mace, with salt and stewe them altogether, and then serue them with the soppes.

TO MAKE EGGES IN MONE SHINE

Take a dishe of rose water, and a dishe full of suger, and set them upon a chafingdish, and let them boile, then take the yolkes of 8 or 9 egges newlaid, and put them thereto, euery one from other, and so let them harden a little, and so after this manner serue them forth, and cast a little Cinnamon and Suger.

TO MAKE AN APPELMOISE

Take a dosyn apples, and either rost or boyle them, and drawe them through a strayner, and the yolkes of three or foure egges withall, and as ye straine them, temper them with three or foure sponefull of damaske (rose) water, if ye will, then take and season it with suger and halfe a dish of swete butter and boyle them upon a chafing dish in a plater, and cast biskets or cinnamon and Ginger upon them, and so serue them forth.

AT A FESTE ROIALL PECOKKES SHALL BE DIGHT IN THIS MANERE

Take and flee off the skynne with the fedurs (feathers), tayle, and the nekke, and the hed thereon; then take the skyn with all the fedurs, and lay hit on a table abrode; and strawe thereon grounden comyn; then take the pecokke, and roste hym, and endore (colour) him with raw yolkes of egges; and when he is rosted take hym of, and let him coole awhile, and take and sowe him in his skyn, and gilde his combe, and so serve him in his skyn, and gilde his combe, and so serve him forthe with the last cours.

This recipe is only included for interest. The peacock is in fact a tough and tasteless bird, and has not the delicacy it was considered to have in former times, but possibly the elaborate methods used in its preparation detracted from its dullness.

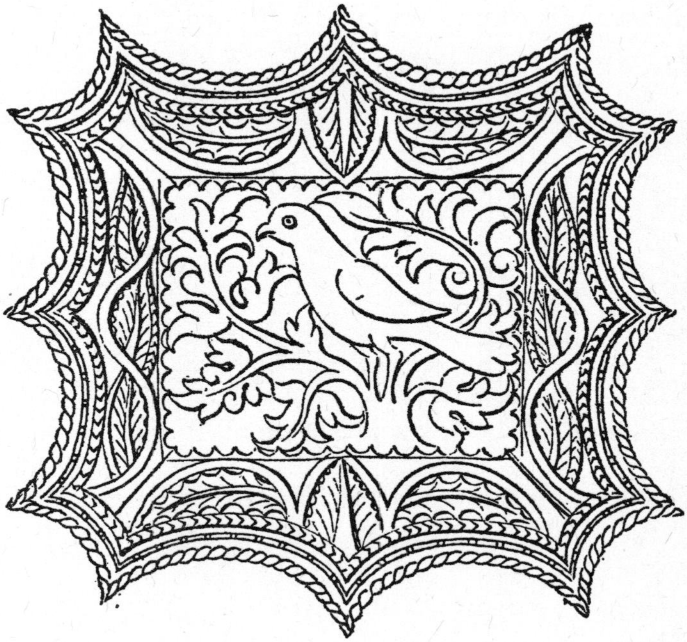

Old English Cookery Glossary

A LA HUGOROTTE Eggs dressed with gravy of roast beef, mushrooms and spices.

ACETARIA Vegetables to eat raw.

ALAY To mix, thicken or temper.

ALAYE To carve or remove the wing (*ail*) of a pheasant.

ALEBURY Ale boiled with sugar, bread and manchet.

ALICANT Spanish wine made from mulberries.

ALKANET The root of a herb which yields a bright red dye, a kind of bugloss.

ALMOND MYLKE or ALMOND MILK Almonds which are blanched, ground and boiled thick with broth, water or wine.

AMYDON Wheat flour, possibly similar to cornflour.

ANEYS or ANIES Aniseed.

ANGELOT A cheese made of rennet curds, first made in Norway and stamped Angelot.

APPLEMOSE or APPLE MOYSE Stewed and sieved apples as done in the fourteenth century. The mose was probably made from apples after they had been pressed for cider. Similar to the modern Danish method of cooking apples.

ARDOLIAN A kind of pudding made of hog's guts and spices.

ARMED Decorated or larded.

ASSAYE The tasting of dishes at the tables of important personages.

ASSAYER A taster. See SEWER.

ASSONE Straight on, straight away, at once, even.

AYRENE, AYREN, EYREN, EYROUN Eggs. By the end of the fourteenth century the words eyroun and egges were both used, for Caxton in 1490 printed: 'What solde a man in thyse doyes now wryte, egges or eyroun.'

BAKE-MEAT Meat pie.

BALNEUM MARIE or BAIN MARIE A pan of hot water into which pans are put to keep them warm.

BANOCHE or BANNUT TREE Walnut.

BARKE The skin of fruit, i.e. pears, apples etc.

BARM YEAST A liquid form, about 2 tablespoonfuls, equal to 1 oz. ordinary yeast.

BASTARDE A sweet wine.

BAXTER A baker, originally female.

BE YNOUGHE Cooked enough.

BEER, SMALL BEER A weak beer.

BEYFE Beef.

BIS Brown bread.

BISHET Bread made of flour, sugar, eggs, caraway seeds and baked.

BITTOURE A bittern, the bird.

BLANCH-MANGER A dish of cream, eggs and sugar, cooked in puff paste.

BLANK-MANGE or BLEWEMANGER or BLAMINGER Not to be confused with the modern blancmange, it is pounded poultry

[111]

with almonds, cream and eggs, bread, sugar and spices. The Turks have a similar recipe.

BLAYNSHE A powder, a powdered spice.

BOIDE Boiled.

BOLAS Bullace, a wild plum, bigger than a sloe.

BOULTER A flour sieve.

BOULTINGHOUSE A flour store where flour could be sieved and sifted.

BRANDRETH An iron tripod or gridiron.

BRAWNE Lean pig meat, ham or gammon.

BRAYE To pound in a mortar, to crush to powder.

BRED Edge.

BREWES or BROWES or BRUES or BROWET or BRUET Bread soaked in gravy; it also means broth, from the French *brouet*, meaning pottage or broth.

BROATH Broth or gravy.

BROCHE A spit or skewer.

BUGLOSS Borage, the herb.

BUTTERED ALE Ale boiled with butter, eggs and sugar.

BYDENE Together.

CABOCHE Cabbage.

CALVER A term for a flounder boiled in wine, vinegar and spices, or crisping a fresh salmon.

CANEL or CANELLE Cassia, Cinnamon.

CAPRICK Wine from Capri.

CARBERRY Gooseberry.

CARBONADE Grilled steak.

CARDEMOME Cardamom.

CAST IT TO POWDER To throw in spices.

CAUDLE A warm drink or gruel made of ale and sugar and sometimes also egg and spice, sometimes oatmeal.

CAWSEBOBY or CAWSEBOBBY Roasted cheese, welsh rarebit.

CHADEL See CHALDRON:

CHAFE To warm or to heat.

CHAFER or CHAFING DISH A portable stove.

CHALDRON or CHAUDRON Part of the entrails of animals, in a spicy sauce.

CHAPPED UP Chopped or minced.

CHAR The flesh or pulp.

CHARDEQUYNCE A conserve of quinces, a kind of marmalade.

CHARGE To press hard, to load.

CHARGEAT Stiff.

CHARGER A large dish.

CHARWARDEN Pears in wine.

CHASTELATAS Little castles; castles of jelly made templewise.

CHEESECAKE A pastry case filled with cheese curds, currants, eggs, spices etc.

CHET or CHEAT Second quality dark coarse bread.

CHEWIT A small pie.

CHIKOYNS Y-SMETE Minced chicken.

CHINE The backbone or breast of fish; ribs or sirloin of meat.

CHIPS A paste made of gum tragacanth, flour and rosewater.

CHIVARDING A pudding, a sort of haggis: hog's gut filled with nutmeg, ginger, pepper and dates, and boiled.

CHOPIN A Scottish measure containing about an English quart. The French chopin is about 1 pint.

CIRYPPE Syrup or sirup.

CITRON A fruit larger than a lemon, less acid and thicker in rind.

CIVEYE Chive sauce.

CLARRY or CLARET WINE Wine made with honey, spices and grapes and strained.

CLARY Wild sage.

CLARYFYED HONY Honey run clear from the comb.

CLOTH OF ESTATE A canopy spread over the high table where the most honoured guests sat.

CLOWES or CLAWYES Cloves, spice.

COCKET Bread which bears a baker's mark as a guarantee of quality.

CODLINGS Green apples for boiling.

COFFIN or COFFYN A pastry case or raised crust for a pie.

COLE Charcoal.

COLE or KAIL Cabbage.

COLEWORTES Cabbage.

COLLAR Something which is half-boiled, rolled up with spices and herbs, then baked in a pot.

COLLOPS Slices of bacon, or bacon and eggs.

COMFITS Long or square pellets of sugar; sweetmeats.

CONNIE or CONIE A rabbit over a year old.

CORIANDER Carminative and aromatic seed.

CORRATES A sort of marmalade.

COSTARD Large cooking apples, probably ribbed.

COUCHE To lay flat.

COYNE A quince.

COYTE Water and yeast.

CRACKNEL A sort of cracker biscuit.

CRUDDES Curds.

CRUSTADE A pie.

CUBBERDER Similar to sideboards in use, they were movable boards on which were placed bread, salt, knives, spoons, drinking vessels etc.

CULLIS A smooth, strong broth, a dissolved jelly.

CULPONE A slice.

CURDS Junket.

CURRANS English red and white currants, also gooseberries.

CURY Not curry but a contraction of the word cookery.

CUSTARD An open pie filled with eggs and milk. After 1600 a custard was baked, as today, without pastry.

CUTE A sweet wine.

CYVES Chives.

DAMASK WATER Rose-water.

DARIOLE An open pie.

DEL Part, some.

DEVIL A dry devil was carbonade (*q.v.*) scored, salted, peppered, mustarded and spiced.

DIGHTE To dress or prepare poultry.

DILLIGROUT A mess of pottage offered to the King of England on Coronation Day by the Lord of the Manor of Addington, Surrey, last served in 1820.

DISWERE Doubt.

DO To put or to add.

DOF Do off.

DORRE To gild or varnish.

DOUCE Sweet.

DOUCET A sweet dish.

DOUSTE To dust.

DOWHZ Dough.

DRAWE To strain through a sieve or to remove the entrails, and to mix.

DRY To pluck or to clean.

DRYF To roll pastry.

DUBANA To array.

DUMPLING A pudding of meat or grated bread, milk, eggs, suet etc., boiled in a cloth.

DYSE Dice.

DYSHE A dish or plate, also a 'dyshe of butter'.

EGGES IN MONESHYNE Fried eggs.

EGRE Sharp, tart, sour.

EGREDOUCE Sweet-sour sauce.

EGRITTS Young herons.

EKE To add.

ELVER Small eel.

ENARM To lard.

ENBANE To ornament, and to baste.

ENDORED Glazed.

ERBES Herbs.

ERBOLAT A dish of herbs and eggs.

ERE THOU MORE DO Before you do anything else.

ERYNGO A root of sea holly, candied and eaten as a sweetmeat.

ESSEX A cheese made of ewe's milk.

ESY Easy.

FAIRE or FAYRE or FEYRE Clean, nice, good.

FAIRING A present on the occasion of a fair, any complimentary gift, especially cakes, gingerbreads and sweets.

FARSURE Stuffing.

FAYRE (FAIRE) WATER Fresh water.

FEABERRY or FEABAS Gooseberry.

FEDER Feather.

FERE or IN FERE Together.

FINING Clarifying.

FLAMPEYNE or FLAMPOYNTE A decorated tart.

FLAPJACK Fried cake made of butter, apples etc.

FLAUNES Pancakes or a kind of tart, cheesecake or custard tart.

FLAWNS Flakes.

FLEE or FLAY Pull off skin.

FLORENTINE A pie, especially with a crust on top only.

FLORISH Garnish.

FOILS Pastry leaves.

FOOL To crush (from *fouler*).

FRENCH BREAD See PUFFE.

FRICASY Varieties of meat boiled in broth.

FROISE or FRAYSE Something fried, e.g. froise of eggs.

FROMENTY Wheat husked and boiled and either served with venison and porpoise, akin to bread sauce, or with sugar, eggs and milk as a sweet dish. Served until George II's time.

FRUNDELL Two pecks.

FUMOSITY Vaporous.

GALENDINE A sauce for roasted fowl made of grated bread, cinnamon, ginger, sugar, claret and vinegar.

GALLIMAUFREY A dish hashed out of odds and ends. A medley, hochepot, hodgepot etc.

GALYNGALE or GALANGAL A substitute or old word for the roots of the sedge, basil or marjoram or orris root.

GALYNTINE Any dish flavoured with galyngale.

GENSBREAD or GENGERBREAD Originally called Gingibreturm, today gingerbread. See page 45.

GIGOT Leg or haunch of mutton or veal; a slice.

GILLYFLOWER A clove-scented pink, mentioned by Markham.

GLAIR The white of egg, and substances of a similar consistency.

GOBBIT A lump of meat the size of a man's thumb.

GODE Strong.

GOURD Vegetable marrow.

GREDELLE Gridiron.

GREENFISH Cod.

GREESE Lard.

GREKE Sweet wine.

GRENE METIS Green vegetables.

GREWEL A kind of broth made of water groats and currants, butter, egg and sugar.

GREYNES DE PRAYS/PARADYS Cardamom.

GUYSE OF BEYONDE THE SEA A stew prepared in a foreign manner.

GYBERNES Gizzard of fowl.

GYNGYNES Ginger.

HAGGAS A gut-filled pudding with minced jelly or with all sorts of things such as eggs, carrots, sugar, herbs and suet.

HAK To cut or chop.

HASLET A piece of meat for roasting.

HASTELER The roasting cook.

HAVERCAKES Oatcakes.

HELDE To pour.

HERYN A hair sieve.

HEWE To cut or chop.

HI They.

HIPPOCRAS A spiced red wine drink said to have been invented by Hippocrates, by dripping it through a sleeve. Wynkyn de Worde gives a recipe for it in his book.

HIT It.

HOATE Hot.

HOCHEE Hache or hash.

HODGEPOT A stew of various meats and vegetables.

HOGSHEAD A cask of varying capacity which in 1491 held 100–140 gallons or possibly $52\frac{1}{2}$ imperial gallons or 63 old wine gallons.

HOLE PARADE To peel or skin whole.

HOLYBUTTE Halibut; literally, holy plaice or flounder, because it was always eaten on holy days.

HOOGOO or HAUTGOUT Something with a high taste, a relish.

HULL To shell.

HURTES Whortleberries.

ICARNE To cut in pieces.

IMELLE Mixed.

IPPOCRAS See HIPPOCRAS

ISOPE Hyssop, a herb.

IWYS Truly.

JACK Half a Yorkshire pint; quarter of a Lincolnshire pint; a machine for turning the spit when roasting meat.

JELLYE Liquid drawn from calves' feet etc., i.e. jelly.

JUMBALLS A kind of sweet bread made of flour, eggs, and cinnamon and made up into rolls or rings.

JUNK A piece or lump, therefore junket or curds.

JUOSHELL A mixture of various things.

KASTE Cast.

KELE or KEELE To cool. To quote Shakespeare: 'While greasy Joan doth keele the pot'.

KERRE To command, instruct, show or direct.

KERVE To carve.

KICKSHAW Various combinations of food, sweet and savoury. Shakespeare makes Justice Shallow order 'some pigeons ... and any pretty kickshaws'. Cromwell abominated them, and Steele had contempt for men 'fed with kickshaws and ragouts'. It is a corruption from the French *quelque chose*.

KILDERKIN A measure of a quarter of a ton or 16–18 gallons.

KNAVE Boy employed as a servant.

LAMPREY A sort of pseudo fish or eel that attaches itself to stones without suckers. *See* pages 12–13, 30.

LARDYS Thin slices.

LATTEN A kind of brass-coloured tin plate used as a material for making utensils.

LAVEROCK Lark.

LAY or LYE To mix.

LEACH or LIECHE Slices, long ones, or the way you serve slices or leaches ('as ye doe lieche'). *See* LESCHE.

LEATHERCOAT A good winter apple, not large but with a good sharp taste – Elizabethan.

LEECHES Strips of meat dressed in sauce or jelly.

LESCHE A slice; also LEACH, a kind of jelly of cream, isinglass, sugar and almonds.

LESE To pick or glean.

LET Milk. Also without or without hindrance.

LICOURE A sauce.

LIMBRECK A vessel used for distillation.

LINKS Sausages.

LIOUR Thickening.

LIRE The fleshy part of meat.

LITE Few.

LIVERING A liver pudding made into a sausage.

LOAF Two manchets (*q.v.*).

LOKE Take care, be sure, look or see.

LONG COFFINS Pies without lids.

LONG PASER Beans.

LONG PIPER A spice.

LONG WORTES A dish similar to bubble and squeak. Also a name for a vegetable, i.e. cole wort, also lettuce or spinach.

LONGWORTES Carrots.

LOVE-APPLE A tomato.

LOZEN A thin pastry cake popular in the fourteenth and fifteenth centuries, sometimes covered with gold for great feasts.

LUCE A pike, especially when fully grown.

LUE To warm.

LUMBER PYE A pie made of minced meat or fish and eggs made in balls and baked in the pastry.

LYE HEM UP To thicken or mix them.

LYN Linen.

LYOURE A mixture.

LYTH or LYTHING Oatmeal or groats for thickening broth.

MA or MAW Fowl.

MAGIRIC Relating to cooking.

MALACHI A fowl 'leached' or sliced.

MALE Galingale.

MALMSLEY A wine strong and sweet; the name is a corruption from Monem Vasia, a Greek town in the Morea, where it was originally made.

MALVIS Mallow.

MANCHET or MANSHET One manchet equals 6 oz.; two manchets equal one loaf; best white bread made into rolls broad in the middle and sharp at the ends.

MARCHPANE A round cake raised at the edges made of ground almonds, sugar and rose-water; also called *massepain* from the French; today's marzipan.

MARGERUM Sweet marjoram.

MARINE To marinate or pickle in a marinade.

MARMELO *See* page 22.

MARY Marrow.

MARYBONYS Marrowbones.

MASLIN or MASSLEDINE Wheat and rye mixed.

MAW Stomach or fowl.

MAWMENE or MAWNONY or MOMENY A sort of pounded poultry or porridge, well spiced.

MAZER A drinking cup with a long stem.

MEAD A fermented (alcoholic) mixture of honey and water and ginger. Other terms are hydromel, metheglin and mulse.

MEDEL To mix.

MELLE To mix.

MENT To mingle.

MESS Helpings of food cut for four people.

MESSE To portion out food; or a portion of food.

METHEGLIN A medicated, spiced variety of mead.

METIS Vegetables.

MORTREWES Dishes made in a mortar and ground to a pulp.

MOT May or must.

MOUNTANCE Amount.

MUNDIFY To cleanse or purify.

MURREY A dark red colour – mulberry.

MUSKADELLE, MUSCADELL, MUSKADINE A sweet wine, strong and spiced and made from muscat or similar grapes. *The Compleat Gardener* (1719) quotes three kinds of muscat grapes, black, red and white.

MUTCHKIN A liquid measure, $\frac{3}{4}$ pint.

MYDDES Midst.

MYED Crumbled or pounded.

MYLTES Spleens.

MYN Less.

MYNTES Mint, the herb.

NAVEN A kind of turnip.

NEAT or NEET Beef, ox or cow.

NECTAR A potent drink of wine, honey, sugar and spices.

NEE *See* page 52.

NEP Cat-mint.

NERE Kidneys.

NESH Soft, tender and juicy.

NOTTYS Walnuts.

NOUMBLES *See* UMBELS.

NYLLE Will not.

NYM Take.

NYS Is not.

OBLES or OBLYS A type of wafer, from the French *oublie*.

OLERA Vegetable for the pot.

OLIA A hodge-podge of several ingredients, of Spanish origin.

OLIVES Beef or mutton in slices with a stuffing of herbs, eggs, and suet, rolled up and roasted or baked.

ONONE At once.

ONYS Ounce.

OPSONY Anything eaten with bread to give it a relish.

OR THAT Till that.

ORENGE PILLES Orange peels.

ORGEATE Originally this meant barley water, later it was flavoured with almonds, and eventually became almond milk.

OSEL or OUSEL A blackbird.

OSEY or OZNEY The name of a sweet French wine, *vin d'Aussey*, from Alsace.

OTHER Or.

OVERBLAUNCHED Blanched.

OVERBOYLED Boiled until it overflows.

PADELLA or PATELLA Frying pan, a word still used in Italy.

PAIN DEMAYN Best white bread, a corruption from *panis Dominicus* (the Lord's bread) because each loaf was impressed with the figure of Christ.

PANTER or PANTLER Before the twelfth century this meant a baker; in the thirteenth century it was one who worked in a pantry.

PAOUS or PAON Peacocks and peahens. Also pakok, pekok, pehenne, pohenne.

PAP Milk and flour boiled together, for invalids or children.

PARYD Pared or peeled.

PAST or PAEST Pie crust.

PASTE-ROYAL also PAEST ROYALL A paste made of flour, sugar, almond milk, butter and eggs, rose-water, saffron and ambergris and musk.

PASTERNACK Parsnip.

PASTLER A maker of pastry.

PAYN Puff or light fritter made in a pan.

PECE A drinking cup.

PECK Two gallons dry measure.

PEEL or PELYS Baker's peel or even a pole for taking things out of the oven.

PEIONS Pigeons.

PELETS Balls.

PEPYNS Pippins.

PERRY Person.

PERSOLE or PARCELLY or PERSELEY Parsley; Hamburg parsley whose roots were also used.

PERYS Pears.

PESON or PESSEN or PEASON or PEASYN Peas. 'Shut the gate after you, I'll tell you the reason, Because the pigs should not get into the peasen'. *A Proper New Boke of Cookerye.*

PESTLE The leg of an animal, e.g. the haunch of venison. Also chicken leg.

PETTY Little.

PETYPANE Marchpane, a purée of pea soup.

PEVRATE SAUCE Pepper sauce for venison.

PILLES Citrus peels or rind.

PIPE 138 gallons.

PITH OF EGGS Egg yolks.

PLACE Plaice.

PLATE Sugared confections.

PLATTER or PLATER A flat dish or wooden plate.

PLAYLAND ON Boiling.

PLY Fold.

PLYACE or PLACE Plaice, usually served with a sorrel sauce.

POME An apple or fruit of the apple kind.

POMECITRON *See* CITRON.

POMEDORRY A dish formed to look like some kind of yellow ball.

POMEGRANATE Made up. A meat ball covered with green (parsley) and yellow batter.

POMPION A large melon or pumpkin.

POOR KNIGHTS PUDDING Slices of bread dipped in eggs, cream and sugar, fried in rose-water and butter. Probably of Norman origin.

PORCELLO Young pigs.

PORRA A kind of porridge.

PORRAYE or PORRAIE A purée, especially of chicken.

PORTINGALE An orange from Portugal.

POSNET or PIPKIN A little pot or skillet.

POSSETT Hot milk poured on alé or sack, having sugar, grated biscuit, eggs and other ingredients boiled in it; a delicacy used for colds and given to bridegrooms.

POSYE A faggot or bouquet of herbs.

POTTELL Two quarts (half a gallon).

POUDER MARCHANT Pulverized spices.

POUDERED or POWDRED Salted, but usually referred to the salting of meat or fish.

POUDRE BLANCHE Cinnamon, ginger, nutmegs and might also mean sugar.

POUDRE DOUCE Cinnamon and sugar but mild.

POUDRES Spices, a name given to several spices.

POWCHE A poached egg.

POWRE To pour.

PRICK Skewer.

PRYMROSE or PRYMEROLE or PRUMAROLE Primrose.

PUFFE A light cake, like bread, also called French bread.

PUFFS Slices of lemon dipped in batter, then fried and sugared.

PUT IT ON or PUTON Pour on it.

PYE Pie.

PYMENT A sweet red wine made with honey and spices added, used in much the same way as liquemo, made by *pignantari* or apothecaries, e.g. Hippocras, Clary.

PYNES *Pignoli*, the Italian pine kernels.

QUAKING PUDDING A pudding made of breadcrumbs, cream, eggs and spices.

QUARE A quarter or a square.

QUARTLE A quart.

QUAYLE The quail, the bird.

QUAYLE or QUAYLING To curdle.

QUEDE Bad.

QUENNELLE From the French, *conil*.

QUERN A handmill for grinding corn, pepper and mustard.

QUESY Cheese.

QUEUERIE The business of queux or cooks.

QUIBIBES A warm spicy grain.

QUIDDANY A thick fruit jelly, thicker than a syrup but not so stiff as marmalade, originally made of quinces. Also called codinac etc., a sort of quaking jelly which could also be made of pippins and plums; it was well sugared and stored in boxes.

QUODLINGS See CODLINGS.

RABETS or RABBITS Suckling rabbits; grown ones were conies.

RAISINS OF THE SUN Sweet raisins from Malaga or muscatels.

RAPE A kind of turnip; also mustard, of the mustard and cress kind.

RAPEY A dish made with grated ingredients.

RASPISE or RASPYS Sweet wine from the unbruised grapes or raspberries.

RAVELED CHEAT A 16-oz. loaf made of wholemeal flour.

RAYSINS COURANCE or CORRANCE or RAYSONS CORRANTE, or SMALL RAYSYNGES or REYSONS All the small grapes growing in the Greek islands and especially prepared as currants.

REARE EGG A soft egg.

REDE To advise.

REFECTION Refreshment, or a refectory, a dining hall.

RENNER Jelly bags through which jelly or wine was poured.

RENSARD This appears to have been the table that received or was awarded the dishes from the high table when the archbishop was done with them.

RERE Late suppers or banquets; or to raise.

RESTY Rancid or mouldy.

RESTYING To become rancid.

RISSHEWS Rissoles.

ROCHET Red gurnard, not a roach.

ROMAN BEAN Haricot bean.

ROMNEY or RUMNEY A sweet table wine, Greek or Hungarian.

ROO Roe deer.

ROOSTED BREDE Toast.

ROPES or ROPPIS Guts.

ROSASOLIS Originally a cordial of the juice of the sundew herb, later made of brandy, sugar and spices, from the mid-sixteenth century to the mid-eighteenth century.

ROSEE A dish flavoured with rose petals.

RUYAN Cheese from Rouen.

RYAL Royal.

RYNE Rhenish wine.

RYNES Skins.

RYPTAGE A Portuguese wine imported into England in the fifteenth century.

RYS Rice.

SACK An amber wine, imported from Jerez, Malaga, Cadiz and Teneriffe during the sixteenth and seventeenth centuries.

SADRON or SAFIRON Saffron.

SAL Usually means in a sauce.

SALLET or SALLETTE Salad.

SALMAGUNDI A dish of meat usually of cold turkey, or a type of mixed meat salad.

SAMBOCADE A fritter flavoured with elder flowers.

SAUNDERS or SAUNDERYS Used for colouring and comes from Sanders Blue, a corruption of the French *cendres bleues*. Saunders also means red sanders wood, not sandalwood with which it is confused.

SAWCE MADAME Goose.

SAWGE Sage.

SCAMLYNGE Days in Lent when no regular meals were provided: Mondays, Saturdays and Ash Wednesday.

SCEARED Sieved or sifted.

SCHERE To cut or shred.

SCHYVES Slices.

SCOTCH To cut it across with a knife before serving.

SEARCER A sieve.

SEETH To boil.

SEKE To plunge or to soak.

SELF Same.

SEWE or SEWEIS A stew or broth, also a sauce or juice.

SEWE To stew, or a broth or sauce; juice, especially onions.

SEWER The officer who sets or removes dishes and who also tasted them at the assaye (*q.v.*).

SEWING or SEWYNGE Assaying or the tasting of food to detect poison.

SHENE Skin.

SHIVES Little round pieces of bread.

SHOES TO MAKE SEWES Stew or broth.

SHOOP Rose-hip.

SHOVELARD An extinct bird.

SILLABUB A syllabub, drink or dish made of cream and wine, sweetened and flavoured, often frothy.

SIMNEL Originally a spice-bread.

SIMPLE A medicament; a herb gathered for medicinal use.

SITHE A sieve, especially for straining milk.

SITHEN Then, since or next.

SITHES Chives.

SKYLSE A flat stick used for beating.

SLAKE Lukewarm.

SLEEPWORT A lettuce.

SLIKED Smoothed.

SMITE Chop.

SMOTHERED Boiled.

SNYTE A snipe (the bird).

SOD Boiled or sodden or pickled.

SOP Bread toasted and seeped in wine, sack or ale.

SOPPES Sippets or bread toasted and soaked in gravy or wine; the name is also applied to a soup with sippets in it.

SOPS-IN-WINE Carnations.

SOTELTYE Sugared table decoration (at the end of a dinner). *See* WARNER.

SOTHYN Boiling.

SOWL Food eaten with bread (meat, cheese etc.); food added to broth.

SPAGYRIC Alchemy.

SPINEE A dish flavoured with hawthorn flowers.

SPITCHCOCK To cut up and cook, especially to cut and boil or fry an eel in breadcrumbs and chopped herbs.

SPORAGE Bean.

SPRYING To sprinkle.

STAMP Grind.

STOCK DOVE Wood pigeon.

STONDYING Thick.

STRENE Scum or to strain.

STRYKE To cut.

SUAND Following.

SUCCACK Fruit preserved in sugar or candied or vegetables (hellice, orange, pumpkin etc.).

SUCCORY Chicory or endive.

SUCKET A sweetmeat, sugar stick.

SUGAR PLATE White sugar, white of eggs, gum tragacanth and rose-water moulded.

SUMDELE Somewhat.

SURNAPPE Napkin.

SWENG To beat up or whip eggs.

SWILK Such.

SWONGEN Beaten up.

SYE To drip, or a strainer, especially for milk. To drain or strain.

SYNAMON Cinnamon.

TALMOUSE A tart or sugared pastry made with cheese, cream and eggs; a sort of cheesecake.

TANSEY Tansy, a herb used to make a sort of fried custard.

TARTEE A compound for filling pastry cases.

TASSATAY TARTS Pastries with apples and spices.

TEMPER To season, to sauce, mix, blend, mingle.

TESE To mince or shred small.

THOMPING Large.

TOD To turn or spread about.

TON TRESSIS Cress.

TORRENTYNE OF EBREW Sweet wine.

TOURTEBREAD Bread made of unboulted meal.

TRAP A dish; or a pastry case.

TRAPE A platter.

TRAUNCHE To slice.

TRE Wooden.

TREADLE The little membrane that holds the yolk of an egg in place.

TREEN Any small household object made of wood.

TRENCHER See page 56.

TRENCHERMAN A cook or a hearty eater.

TRIFLE Junket.

TRIPES Belly of beef.

TRUSS The process of dressing of fowl.

TRY or TRYID Pick, pull, broken up, separated.

TURNESOLE A colour for jelly. Some say it is turmeric, others *croten tinctorum*; also from heliotrope.

TURTLE An abbreviation for turtle-dove.

TWEYDEL Twice.

TYRE A sweet wine.

UMBLES The entrails of a deer. As this was only served at lower table, it gave birth to the saying 'eating humble pie'.

UNCE Ounce.

UNTACH To loosen, from the French *detacher*.

URCHINS Hedgehogs.

USQUEBAUGH Gaelic for whisky.

VAUNTE A type of fritter.

VAUTES To vault. Roughly it means to turn in the pan.

VERDE SAUCE A green sauce.

VERJUICE or VERGIS or VERGIOUS or VERGYE A sour juice made from crab-apples, sour apples, unripe grapes or gooseberries. Sometimes fermented but not vinegar.

VERMOUTH See WORMWOOD.

VERNAGE A strong sweet Italian wine, red or white, produced in Tuscany.

VERNAGELLE A sweet white wine.

VIANT Meat.

VIANT FRITURE Meat fritter.

VOIDER or VOYDER A tray or basket into which scraps were put as the table is cleared.

VOYD Clear.

VYNNES Fins.

WAFER A thin biscuit or leaf of pastry. See page 42.

WALM A short period of boiling up liquor.

WARDEN A kind of pear like a spotted quince. See page 33.

WARLICHE Warily.

WARNER A tart or cake or confection made of sugar and paste, built into an elaborate decoration carried around before a course at dinner; probably like a wedding cake decoration, only larger.

WASTEL White bread made of fine flour, or sometimes a cake with honey.

WELLE To boil.

WHITEMEAT Eggs, butter and cheese.

WHITEPOT A custard in a pastry case made

from cream, eggs, apple, sugar, mace, cinnamon and sippets of bread.

WHOT Hot.

WINE CUTE Sweet wine.

WONE Quantity.

WORMWOOD *Artemesia absinthia*, used for flavouring in absinthe and vermouth.

WORTES Vegetables or herbs for cooking.

YEUT or YKUT or YSMETE Minced or finely chopped.

YF If.

YFERE Together.

YNONS Onions.

YNOUGH Enough.

YPOCRAS *See* HIPPOCRAS.

YRCHONS Hedgehogs.

YSOPE Hyssop, the herb.

YT That.

Y'TRYID Separated yolks of egg.

Illustration Acknowledgments

The Editor and publishers of this book wish to thank the following for permission to reproduce pictures from the books and manuscripts listed below.

THE TRUSTEES OF THE BRITISH MUSEUM

The Canterbury Tales, *Geoffrey Chaucer, 1498*, p. 35
Livre de Prouffitz Champêtres, *1529*, p. 11
Banket der Hofe und Edelleut, *Lobera de Avila, 1556*, pp. 13, 23, 123
Opera di M. Bartolemo Scappi cuoco secreto di Papa Pio V, *B. Scappi, 1570*, pp. 51, 60
The Ordinary of the Company of Bakers in the City of York, (*Add. 34605 f24v–25*), c. *1596*, endpapers
Opera dell'Arte di Cucinare, *B. Scappi, 1622*, pp. 10, 26, 66
A Perfect School of Instructions for the Officers of the Mouth, *G. Rose, 1682*, p. 74
Le Vrai Cuisinier François, *F. P. de La Varenne, 1699*, pp. 24, 37, 76
Il Trinciente di M. Vicenzo Cervio, *V. Cervio, 1697*, pp. 84, 85
E. Kidder's Receipts of Pastry and Cookery, *1740*, pp. 16, 110
Ballads in the Roxburgh Collection, pp. 25, 41, 86
A History of Domestic Manners and Sentiments during the Middle Ages, *T. Wright, 1862*, pp. 39, 55
Iron and Brass Implements of the English House, *J. Seymour Lindsay, 1927*, pp. 44, 62

CAMBRIDGE UNIVERSITY LIBRARY

Gringoire's Castel of Labours, *1506*, p. 57

RAYMOND OLIVER

Singulier Traicte, sixteenth century, p. 20

All of these, except those on p. 20 and the endpapers, are reproduced from photographs taken by John Freeman.

Select Bibliography

Antiquitates Culinariae, *Rev. R. Warner, 1791.*
The Art of Cookery, *Poem by W. King, 1706.*
The Art of Dining, *A. Hayward, 1852.*
The Babees Book, *F. J. Furnivall, N. Trübner & Co., London, 1868.*
Book About the Table, *J. C. Jeaffreson, Hurst & Blackett, London, 1875.*
The Closet of the Eminently Learned Sir Kenelme Digbie, *edited by Anne Macdonell, Philip Lee Warner, 1910.*
The Compleat Housewife, *E. Smith, 1750.*
Cooking Through the Centuries, *J. R. Ainsworth-Davis, Dent, London, 1931.*
The Delectable Past, *Esther B. Aresty, Allen & Unwin, London, 1965.*
Delightes for Ladies, *Sir Hugh Plat, Humfrey Lownes, London, 1609.*
A Dictionary of Gastronomy, *André Simon and Robin Howe, Nelson, London, 1970.*
Eagle Foundry Book, *George Swinford.*
England in Tudor Times, *L. F. Salzman, Batsford, London, 1926.*
The English at Table, *J. Hampson, Collins, London, 1944.*
The Englishman's Food, *J. C. Drummond and Anne Wilbraham, Jonathan Cape, London, 1939.*
The English Medieval Feast, *William E. Mead, Allen & Unwin, London, 1931.*
English Social History, *G. M. Trevelyan, 1948.*
The English Table in History and Literature, *Charles Cooper, Sampson Low, Marston & Co., London.*
Filkins Museum Notes.
Food – How Things Developed, *Molly Harrison, Educational Supply Association, London.*
Food in England, *Dorothy Hartley, Macdonald & Co., London, 1964.*
The Forme of Cury, *edited by Samuel Pegge, 1780.*

From Kitchen Yesterdays, *Allan Jobson, Country Life, 1952.*
Gastronomy of the School for Good Living, *1822.*
Geffrye Museum Notes.
Good Cheer, *Frederick Hackwood, Fisher Unwin, 1911.*
Good Fare and Cheer of Old England, *Joan Parry Dutton.*
A History of Everyday Things in England, *Marjore and C. H. B. Quennell, Batsford, London, 1920.*
Homes of Other Days; History of Domestic Manners, *Thomas Wright, 1812.*
Host and Guest, *A. W. Kirwen.*
The Household Roll of Eleanor the Countess of Leicester, *1265.*
Iron and Brass Implements of the English House, *J. Seymour Lindsay.*
Kettner's Book of the Table, *A Manual of Cookery, Dulau & Co., London, 1912.*
Kitchen and Table, *Colin Clair, Abelard - Schuman, 1964.*
Life and Work of the People of England, *Dorothy Hartley.*
The Literature of Cookery, *Col. Kenny Herbert, National Review, 1895, January and August.*
Mrs Beaton, *1861.*
A Noble Boke off Cookry ffor a Prynce Houssolde, *Mrs Napier, 1882.*
Northumberland Household Book, *1512.*
Old Cookery Books, *W. Carew Hazlitt, 1886.*
Old English Household Life, *Gertrude Jekyll, Batsford, London, 1925.*
The Original, *Thomas Walker, 1838.*
Pantropheon, *Alexis Soyer, 1853.*
The Pleasures of the Table, *G. H. Ellwanger, Heinemann, London, 1902.*
The Polite World, *Joan Wildeblood and Peter Brinson.*
A Proper New Booke of Cokerye, *edited by Catherine F. Frere, W. Heffer & Sons, Cambridge, 1913.*
Sir Kenelm Digby, *R. T. Petersson, Cape, London, 1956.*
Tudor Food and Pastimes, *Life at Ingatestone Hall, F. G. Emmison, Benn, London, 1964.*

OTHER BOOKS IN THE SERIES

Single-subject Cookery Books
BAKERY, CAKES AND SIMPLE CONFECTIONERY Maria Floris
CHEESE AND CHEESE COOKERY T. A. Layton
CLASSIC SAUCES AND THEIR PREPARATION Raymond Oliver
EGGS Margaret Sherman
HERBS, SPICES AND FLAVOURINGS Tom Stobart
MEAT Ambrose Heath
POULTRY AND GAME Robin Howe
SOUPS Robin Howe
SWEET PUDDINGS AND DESSERTS Margaret Sherman

Regional Cookery Books
FAR EASTERN COOKERY Robin Howe
THE FRENCH AT TABLE Raymond Oliver
GERMAN COOKERY Hans Karl Adam
JEWISH COOKERY Madeleine Masson
SPANISH COOKERY Mary Hillgarth

Wine Books
THE COMMONSENSE OF WINE André L. Simon
GODS, MEN AND WINE William Younger
THE WINES OF BORDEAUX Edmund Penning-Rowsell
THE WINES OF BURGUNDY H. W. Yoxall

Titles in Preparation
TRADITIONAL BRITISH COOKERY Malpas Pearse
FISH COOKERY Jane Grigson
REGIONAL FRENCH COOKERY Ken Toye
REGIONAL ITALIAN COOKERY Robin Howe
THE GAZETTEER OF WINES André L. Simon
SCANDINAVIAN COOKERY Tore Wretman

THE INTERNATIONAL WINE AND FOOD SOCIETY

The International Wine and Food Society was founded in 1933 by André L. Simon, C.B.E., as a world-wide non-profit-making society.

The first of its various aims has been to bring together and serve all who believe that a right understanding of wine and food is an essential part of personal contentment and health; and that an intelligent approach to the pleasures and problems of the table offers far greater rewards than the mere satisfaction of appetite.

For information about the Society apply to the Secretary, Marble Arch House, 44 Edgware Road, London W2

He that giveth measure,   It maketh a poore man,
God blesse the with treasure.   To sell flower for bran.

Looke well to thy season,   Be iust with thy weightes
With conninge and reason.   God plague falle weightes.

Who so followethe theis preceptes well,